People who hurt are people on stretchers. To hurt is bad enough, but to hurt alone destroys people—physically, mentally and spiritually.

The knowledge of this truth has led me to engage in this practical ministry called stretcher bearing—the ministry of encouragement and support.

It means so much to me, and I want it to mean as much to you.

So grab a handle.
Grab a handle?
That's right. Grab a handle. Let's get started.
Who? Me?
Yes, you! Okay, lift!
But how?
How? Have you never been a stretcher bearer before?
No. Do I even have the potential to grab the handle of someone's stretcher?
Yes, if you believe in the concept of stretcher bearing. What are your feelings about being a stretcher bearer?
I don't know for sure.
Let's talk about it.

THE
STRETCHER

BRINGING HEALING AND HOPE
TO A BROKEN AND HURTING WORLD

MICHAEL SLATER

Formerly published under the titles *Becoming A Stretcher Bearer* and *Stretcher Bearer*.

Published by Stretcher Bearer Ministries, La Habra, CA.

Cover design and layout by Rafael Polendo (polendo.net)
Cover images © mike_experto / Fotolia

Printed in the U.S.A.

DEDICATION

This book is dedicated to my wife Gilda, who has been an encourager and stretcher-bearer to me. She never doubted that the Lord would open the door to the theme of stretcher-bearers becoming a book. With much love, I dedicate this book to her.

A few days later, when Jesus again entered Capernaum, the people heard that he had come home. So many gathered that there was no room left, not even outside the door, and he preached the word to them. Some men came, bringing to him a paralytic, carried by four of them. Since they could not get him to Jesus because of the crowd, they made an opening in the roof above Jesus and, after digging through it, lowered the mat the paralyzed man was lying on.

When Jesus saw their faith, he said to the paralytic, "Son, your sins are forgiven."

Now some teachers of the law were sitting there, thinking to themselves, "Why does this fellow talk like that? He's blaspheming! Who can forgive sins but God alone?"

Immediately Jesus knew in his spirit that this was what they were thinking in their hearts, and he said to them, "Why are you thinking these things? Which is easier: to say, 'Get up, take your mat and walk?' But that you may know that the Son of Man has authority on earth to forgive sins…" He said to the paralytic, "I tell you, get up, take your mat and go home."

He got up, took his mat and walked out in full view of them all. This amazed everyone and they praised God, saying, "We have never seen anything like this!"

– Mark 2:1-12

CONTENTS

FOREWORD

We all feel it. That strange mixture of worry and concern about people. Some are troubled, ill or distressed. Others lack self-esteem and need our affirmation, while others are battling self-incrimination over some failure and reach out for forgiveness and love. Still others face seemingly impossible problems and cry out for us to give understanding and encouragement. And then there are those who yearn to pull out all the stops and need us to be their cheerleader to spur them on.

For these and so many others we long to know how to be the quality of caring friend they need so desperately. We can understand the need. We need friends like that ourselves! Most of all, our deepest desire is to put people in touch with the Master. We pray eventually and discover that part of His answer is to use us as His agents of love and hope. Then we experience again that the joy of the Christian life is to be to others what He has been to us. We are filled with awe and wonder that He has called us to be His friends and wants to enable us to be liberating friends to others. How to do that in the most creative way is our urgent concern.

That's why I'm so excited about this book by Mike Slater. Believing that a true friend is someone who is always there when it matters, when it counts, when it hurts, Mike leads us into profound biblical meaning of friendship with Christ and one another. To be in Christ means to be in ministry. And that ministry begins within the Christian fellowship where we are called to set each other free to live at full potential in the difficulties and delights of life.

In his warm, direct manner, Mike challenges us, as Christians, to look deep within ourselves at our motivations, at our priorities, at our involvement with others. And with a disarming, yet urgent sincerity, he compels us also to look hard at our contemporary life-styles – with the false bravado, rugged individualism, painful isolation and other alienating attitudes that estrange us from one another.

Mark 2 is the account of a paralyzed man fortunate enough to have four loving, compassionate friends who were also men of great faith. They acted on their faith and carried their paralyzed friend to Jesus. "When Jesus saw their faith" – the faith of the four stretcher-bearers – He acted on their faith and healed their crippled friend on the spot.

Acting on our faith with love and compassion for others – ministering to others with the gift of encouragement and support – that is the ministry of stretcher bearing.

If you believe God is calling you to such a ministry, then Stretcher Bearers was written for you. As you read, be open to God's leading as He directs you into a creative ministry of encouragement and support among those God brings into your life. And then watch God act miraculously in their lives because you first acted in faith yourself.

God bless you, stretcher-bearer!

— DR. LLOYD JOHN OGILVIE

PREFACE

Years ago I attended a retreat held for ministers and church-related lay people. This event took place at a time in my life when I was trying to decide if God truly was calling me into the ministry.

At this retreat I took the time to observe closely other men and women who already had responded to the call of God and were now actively involved in church work. The longer I watched these people, the more I wondered if I were being called to become a pastor. Why? Because I felt a great difference between my life and theirs.

From what I could observe, none of these men and women appeared to have any problems. Nothing ever seemed to go wrong in their lives. And from their comments, it was obvious they spent a great deal of time praying for other people. Yet they appeared not to need prayer support for themselves. My conclusion then was that they had no disappointments, heartaches, tensions or problems.

To me, the people I observed were spiritual giants – spiritual giants who were able to deal with all of life's issues and who seemed never to experience hurt or need. I began to compare myself with them. Did I have what it takes to be a pastor? I was painfully aware of the times I hurt, the times I cried, the times I doubted and the times I needed help. Could such a person as I was, with such personal needs, be called into the ministry?

As I thought more deeply about pastors, the Church and the Christian community as a whole, I began to realize that many of us are indeed living out a peculiar kind of Christian philosophy. This philosophy says we do not need one another, that everything is going great and that it's the "other person," never ourselves, who has needs. This realization almost discouraged me from the pastorate because I knew my life definitely was not without need.

Perhaps it was this very acknowledgment that reversed my thought, for at the same moment, I found myself not only certain of God's call to the ministry, but I was assured also that there was a dimension of Christianity I wanted to help believers to grasp. That dimension – the practice of the gift of encouragement and support – is what I now call stretcher bearing. And those who practice it are stretcher-bearers.

A second incident at a second conference had a further impact upon my thinking and, therefore, upon my own self-worth. Attending a youth conference as a young minister of youth, I was in awe of some of the other ministers present. Men and women whom I respected, they were spiritual heroes to me and inspirations to me in my ministry.

One morning one of these men came up to me and said, "I would love the privilege of getting together with you. How about over a Coke this afternoon?" He felt we needed some special time to get to know one another better.

I couldn't' believe what I had heard. This successful, highly regarded man wanted to sit down with me? With me? Why? I felt both honored and scared. Why would he want to take his time and spend it with a young youth minister?

That afternoon we did get together over Cokes and had a great time getting to know each other. I can't recall all that this man shared with me, but I do remember one statement he made that has stayed with me as a real source of encouragement.

As our conversation came to a close he looked straight into my eyes and said, "Michael, I want to tell you something. This afternoon I'm buying stock in you as a person and as a minister. Right now, as you begin your ministry, the stock is not 'at a high.' But one day stock in you is going to pay big dividends, and I'm buying into it right now, because I believe in you and in your response to the plan God has for your life."

Here was a man with years of successful ministry, not yet knowing me closely, yet willing, not only to sit down and have a Coke with me, but also willing to risk himself. He said, "I believe in your right now as you begin, even as you experiment and as you grow toward being the man the Lord intends you to be."

That afternoon as I walked alone among the pines, I prayed, "Lord, what is this all about? What can the words of this good man mean? Were they words from you? Were they the inspiration and encouragement you know I needed to hear? Will the stock pay off and will there be dividends years down the road?"

Over and over in my mind I kept hearing that phrase, "I'm buying stock in you now, and one day it's going to pay big dividends...I'm buying stock in you and one day it's going to pay big dividends."

Now, years later, this incident, along with many others, brings to mind the realization that God placed certain people in my life to be a source of encouragement and support both to my ministry and to me personally. In the last few years I have been able to give a name to these special people in my life. I call them stretcher-bearers, those encouragers and supporters God uses in the lives of others.

To affirm the stretcher-bearer concept has become a vital part of my life, and my desire is to teach others how to become stretcher-bearers themselves. As a pastor, I am called upon to listen, counsel and advise. My ministry to people in various situations has enabled me to understand the reasons behind what destroys people today. Individuals have actually come into my office and told me such things as, "No one cares about me. No one cares if I live or if I die." "I go to church regularly, but it seems no one even cares if I am there or if I will ever return."

To hurt is bad enough, but to hurt alone destroys people physically, mentally and spiritually. The knowledge of this truth has led me to engage in this practical program of ministry called stretcher bearing – the ministry of encouragement and support. It means so much to me, and I want it to mean as much to you.

Try to visualize and understand in a deeper way why you need this ministry in your own life. Learn, too, why people don't reach out to be encouraged. You will find in this book practical suggestions and practical advice concerning the gift of encouragement and support. Keep the image of a stretcher ever before you as your read these pages. It is my prayer that stretcher bearing becomes as meaningful in your life as it has in my own.

— MIKE SLATER

ACKNOWLEDGEMENTS

As I look back on the journey of the theme of stretcher-bearers from concept to book, I see clearly the road it has taken toward publication. I have only beautiful memories of the people who were involved with me along the way, and I want to take this opportunity to thank all those who have done so much to support and encourage the writing of this book.

To Joyce Young, who took the thoughts and dreams of stretcher-bearers, and put them on paper in a way no one else could: Words cannot express how much I appreciate all your work and effort on the book. Without you it might never have been written. Your positive spirit and willingness to assist came into my life at a perfect moment. God bless you, Joyce, and our Lord will use mightily the words you helped put within this book.

To Bob Hunt: What can I say? You came along side of me at a time when I was on a stretcher. You lifted me and the ministry with belief, encouragement, support and wisdom. Our friendship goes back many years and continues to reconnect. Without you and the Lord putting us back together, I would not be writing these words of thankfulness. You are a great man of God who encourages and lifts so many. Thank you for lifting me and leading the way to getting this book re-printed. Forever will I be grateful and thankful.

To Rafael Polendo Jr: I have known you since you were a young child. I have watched you grow into a young man of God. With your growth has come many talents. You have graciously come along side of me and Stretcher Bearer Ministries using your talents and time to redesign and layout the book, *The Stretcher*. The cover design is phenomenal. The end results show how gifted you are. Thank you Junior. I will always be a Pastor and friend to you.

Finally, to my church family. You have been a church which allowed me to experiment and implement these thoughts and ideas of stretcher bearing. I have watched so many of you in your loving way lift the stretchers of others who are hurting, and I know you have lifted my own many times. Through many of you I realized the importance of this theme and, therefore, became encouraged to share it with others.

To all of you, I thank you so much for your encouragement. You made the road toward publication enjoyable, meaningful and well worth the effort. I love you all.

ONE

THE FIRST STRETCHER BEARERS

Eleazar looked out through the door of his house at the rapidly gathering crowd and shook his head in amazement. "We're besieged already, and Jesus has only just arrived," he exclaimed. And then, to no one in particular, he asked, "What will it be like out there by the time Jesus begins to speak?"

Word of Jesus' return to the city that day had spread quickly throughout all Capernaum. "Jesus is back. He's staying at Eleazar's house." And now, though it was still early in the day, the first eager arrivals had already assembled as close to the house as they could get. Some had come out of friendship, for James and John – Zebedee's sons – and Andrew and Peter, all sons of Capernaum, had returned home with Jesus. Others had come in expectation of what Jesus would say, and the curious ones had come in hopes of seeing a miracle.

Typical of most homes in Capernaum, Eleazar's modest house was a single-story, boxlike affair with a door, two windows and a flat, mud-covered roof made of branches and straw. Steps were built into an outside wall of the house, so someone could climb up and repair the damage whenever the mud of the roof eroded. The steps also allowed the family to enjoy the comfort of the rooftop in the cool of the evening after a hot, tiring day.

Across the city from Eleazar lived five men – Barnabas, Stephen, Matthias, Philip and Nicolas. Lifelong companions, the five men enjoyed working together, watching soccer games in Jerusalem or picnicking by the sea with their families. Any plans they made always included Nicolas, even though he – stricken by a paralysis in his youth – could not walk. Always willing to help, Nicolas' friends managed to get him anywhere he needed to go.

Soon after Jesus reached Capernaum that day, the news of His arrival reached Stephen's side of the city. Stephen had already heard of Jesus and the miracles He had performed. He knew that Jesus had been healing people in the various places He visited. And now he was in Capernaum. Stephen paused and thought. *And what about Nicolas? Jesus could surely heal him too.*

Stephen dropped what he was doing and rushed off to round up Barnabas, Matthias and Philip. "Come with me to Nicolas' house," he urged excitedly.

"Why? What's up?" Philip asked.

"I'll explain on the way," Stephen answered. "Let's get going." En route, he explained his plan for them to take Nicolas to Jesus. "We can take our friend, put him on a stretcher and carry him over to the house where Jesus is. I know when Jesus sees Nicolas, He will heal him."

Barnabas was willing, but doubtful. "I don't know," he said. "The crowd will probably be too big."

"Do we even know which house it is or where it is?" Matthias challenged. "We don't want to haul poor Nicolas all over the city," he cautioned.

"No, I don't know exactly which house it is, but if we go, sooner or later we're bound to find the crowd." Stephen answered. "We can figure everything out as we go along. I know we can do it, but we must do it right away. So come on. Here is Nicolas' house now."

Contagious in their excitement, the four friends explained their plan to Nicolas. He was touched by their concern and buoyed by their enthusiasm as they lifted him onto a stretcher. His wife fought to hold back her tears as she watched them go out the door and start across the city. Did she dare hope her husband would be healed and come walking back to her?

Up one cobblestone street and down another the little group trudged. The dustier unpaved streets left them all coughing. Still willing, but weary, the bearers began murmuring.

"These houses all look the same."

"And we don't even have the address."

"Maybe we should just forget the whole thing."

But as full of determined hope as ever, Stephen called over his shoulder. "We're not going to give up now." He looked down at Nicolas and grinned. Stephen's words and example gave the others renewed energy.

Finally, emerging from a winding side street, they found themselves at the rear of an enormous throng of people. The marvelous feeling of having arrived at the right place was nearly choked off by the sight of the multitude.

"Look at that crowd," Barnabas wailed. "We'll never get near the place."

"Even if we did," Matthias pointed out, "It's wall-to-wall people inside. We could never get in there."

The joyful prospect of Nicolas healed and walking again had brought them there. But now it seemed so hopeless. Looking down at their friend on the stretcher, Stephen expressed their momentary disappointment. "Nicolas, we tried. Honest. But we can't get near. Maybe next time."

"Wait," Philip interjected. "We're already here and we're not going to give up now."

Philip stood, studying the crowd. He stroked his beard as he pondered the situation. *There has to be a solution somewhere in all this*, he thought. His eyes roamed over the sea of heads before him to the house itself and came to rest on the steps. He glanced toward the roof.

"That's it! That's it!" he cried. "I've just figured it out. I know what we can do to get Nicolas inside that house to see Jesus."

"What? How?"

Philip quickly took charge. "Stephen, you and I are the biggest. We'll take the front of the stretcher. Matthias, you and Barnabas take the rear. Let's push our way through the crowd and make for the steps. We're taking Nicolas up on the roof. As we pass one of the windows, you guys notice where Jesus is standing inside the house. That's all we need to worry about now. I'll explain the rest when we get up on the roof."

Stephen and Philip gently but firmly shouldered their way through the crowd. Forcing their way through the mass of humanity was slow going, but voicing. "Excuse us, please" at every step; they slowly made their way to the foot of the stairs. As they worked their way through the press of people, the crowd parted briefly and immediately closed behind them.

"I see Him," one of the five whispered, as they passed a window.

Panting with the others from their exertion of getting Nicolas onto the roof, Philip detailed his plan. "We know now where Jesus is standing, right? Well, all we have to do is take our knives and cut a hole through this dried mud and then lower Nicolas down in front of Jesus, right into that space where He is standing now. Okay?"

The men became excited all over again until Barnabas reminded them, "We have no rope. So how in the world are we going to lower the stretcher? We can't just drop Nicolas through the hole. He'd be hurt."

"Hey, that's no problem," Matthias answered. "There are four of us, and we're all wearing sashes. Look," he pointed out, unwinding his own sash. "When you unwrap them, these sashes are at least six feet long. All we have to do is tie a sash to each corner of the stretcher. When we lower it through the roof and add the length of our arms, we'll be able to reach at least eight feet. That will be almost perfect for us to place you right before Jesus, Nicolas," he added, hugging their paralyzed friend.

Barnabas rushed to pace off the roof. "Let's see. Jesus was about 15 feet inside the door, so that would place Him about here."

"Yes, but go about three feet to your left," Stephen suggested. Barnabas began sidestepping,. "There, that's the right spot," Stephen said. The rest agreed, and the four of them zealously started gouging at the roof with their knives.

Meanwhile, inside the house Jesus preached to Eleazar and his family and to all who had managed to squeeze themselves into the small structure. He barely had room to move about as He spoke. All listened intently as Jesus addressed them.

A few moments earlier, Eleazar had been baffled by loud sounds overhead, but was glad no one else seemed to notice. But now dust began falling from the ceiling. He turned to his wife in embarrassment. "I knew I should have patched that roof last week. But I put it off and now bits of it are falling on our guests. It's too late to do anything now. We'll just have to make our apologies afterwards."

Eleazar tried to retain his natural dignity and concentrate on what Jesus was saying. But now his embarrassment was turning to mortification. More dust and dirt was falling than before, and most of it was falling on Jesus. Jesus was coming to the end of His message, and as chunks of dirt and debris fell around Him, He calmly brushed off what He could and continued to speak.

By this time, the noise of the digging and the falling debris could not be ignored. The crowd inside stirred and tried to move away from the rain of mud and straw. All now stared at the ceiling in wonderment. Even Jesus looked up to see what was happening.

The shower of debris stopped and sunlight poured into the room through an opening some three feet wide and seven feet long. A great portion of the ceiling was gone. Four faces appeared first in the gaping hole, and then a stretcher attached to sashes was slowly lowered to the floor below.

Holding his head and rocking back and forth in humiliation, Eleazar exclaimed, "I can't believe it. I can't believe it. First, someone tears a hole in my roof. And now a body comes through the hole. Someone please tell me this isn't happening."

The crowd buzzed with conversation. Some were amused by the proceedings. A few were offended for Eleazar's sake. All were curious as to what was taking place before them.

The crowd wondered if Jesus would be offended by this unconventional entrance. But, as Eleazar looked upon the amused expression and gentle smile of Jesus, he sensed friendship and affirmation. All fear and unrest vanished and a feeling of peace swept over him.

But even before Jesus' eyes rested upon Nicolas, they had looked first into the faces of the four friends watching from above. He had seen love in their faces. But, He had also seen faith. And in response to their faith, he turned to Nicolas and healed him.

As Jesus commanded Nicolas to rise and walk, he felt the marvelous healing of His words go through his body. Never doubting that he had been healed. Nicolas climbed off the stretcher and stood up. For the first time in more years than anyone could remember, he took his first steps.

Bedlam broke loose in the house. The four friends, looking down through the damaged roof, shouted for joy. With tears pouring down their faces, they danced and hugged one another unashamedly.

"Nicolas is healed. Nicolas is healed. Jesus has healed our friend. He has healed our friend. We knew He could do it, and He did!"

In Mark 2:1-12, as in any other story or parable of the Bible, what is important is not that a healing or miracle took place. No, there is more than that. What is important is what the Bible is trying to teach us concerning that miracle or parable.

You see, I believe every miracle in the Bible is there to teach us about a concept of the Christian faith. If we then understand the concept behind the teaching of the miracle – and sometimes it has to do with healing – then the miracle or the concept can take place in our lives today.

What then is the basis of the story in Mark 2:1-12 about the four men carrying their friend on the stretcher? It is this: the paralytic man truly needed his wonderfully determined friends to carry him and his problem to the feet of Jesus. If we understand this concept then the miracle that took place in Mark 2 can take place in your life, in my life, and in the lives of many of our friends.

I repeat, the healing that took place in this account occurred, not primarily because of the man on the stretcher, nor because Jesus had the gift to heal. The healing took place because of the faith, encouragement and support of the man's four devoted friends. They were determined to carry his stretcher, they were determined to find the answers to each problem as it arose: finding the home, knowing where and how to cut the hole in the roof, and then even taking part of themselves – their sashes- and lowering their friend right in front of Jesus. Jesus vividly saw their faith, and he used their faith to give healing to the man on the stretcher.

Sometimes situations make stretcher bearing seem hopeless. That's why stretcher-bearers – yes, and roof cutters, too – need that imaginative faith that turns problems into challenges because the welfare of a friend is involved. A stretcher-bearer is that "friend who sticks closed than a brother" (Prov. 18:24). A stretcher-bearer is that person of encouragement and support who stands by the side of a friend no matter the difficulty.

Mark 2:1-12 gives the biblical understanding of the stretcher-bearer concept. It makes use of a very visual metaphor – a stretcher. Here were four friends, caring for someone who was on such a stretcher. This particular story deals with physical illness, yet people can be on stretchers for a number of reasons: physical illness, social, spiritual or even emotional illness. We need to be prepared for that time when God may call us to lift someone's stretcher.

Each one of us at any moment in life can suddenly be placed on a stretcher, unable alone to deal effectively with a problem. In such moments, we will need to have stretcher-bearers, people sharing the gift of encouragement and support with us.

When I was that young youth minister so many years ago, I had questioned whether or not I had what it took to be a minister of the Gospel of Jesus Christ. A good man pulled me aside at the age of 20, took the time to have a Coke with me and tell me, "Mike, I'm buying stock in you right now in the beginning of your ministry. One day it's going to pay big dividends, but I'm buying it today, not later, because I believe in you." I was on a stretcher then and now I realize that God put that certain stretcher-bearer into my life just at the moment I really needed it.

The stretcher-bearers. A wonderful ministry that is meant to be used in your life and one where God can use you in the lives of others.

As believers, we are well aware that Jesus was wonderfully unique. God gave Him powers that enabled Him to carry out His message and ministry in various ways.

A MIGHTY GIFT WITHIN JESUS

In the course of His earthly ministry Jesus used the full potential of all His various gifts. Think now on what these various gifts were and (1) list what you consider were His seven main gifts in the space provided on this page. Then (2) write down which of all seven you consider to be the most outstanding gift Jesus used in His earthly ministry.

1.
2.
3.
4.
5.
6.
7.

Jesus' most outstanding gift _____

My own answers appear at the end of this chapter, but do not refer to them until you have written your own answers first. *After comparing lists, we will probably find that there are many answers for each question, with justification for each answer given. In my own list I wrote that "encouragement and support" were Jesus' most outstanding gifts. Let me share with you the reasons for my choice.

Has there ever been anyone else like Jesus, who personally and deliberately sought out others just so He could encourage them? As you recall stories and incidents in the Bible, picture the woman caught in adultery and how she was encouraged to, "Go," leave her sinful life behind and start anew (see John 8:1-11). These words liberated her and freed her from the bondage of her past. In other words, she was given a second chance. A chance to start over again, to be forgiven and to make something positive out of her life. Where would any of us be today without a second chance?

Consider the special attitude Jesus had toward children. In Matthew 18:1-6 we read, "At that time the disciples came to Jesus and asked, "Who is the greatest in the kingdom of heaven?" He called a little child and had him stand among them. And he said: 'I tell you the truth, unless you change and become like little children, you will never enter the kingdom of heaven. Therefore, whoever humbles himself like this child is the greatest in the kingdom of heaven. And whoever welcomes a little child like this in my name welcomes me. But if anyone causes one of these little ones who believe in me to sin, it would be better for him to have a large millstone hung around his neck and be drowned in the depths of the sea.'"

He had such a compassionate love for children. He knew that valuable lessons could be learned by showing others how children ought to be treated. We need to understand that, in the days of Jesus, children were not highly regarded. Yet, through His support they were elevated to heights of importance as never before.

Women too did not hold a place of honor in public due to Jewish customs. Think about the times when Jesus talked with women and the loving attitude He had toward them. What an encouragement He was to the woman at the well (see John 4:1-26) and to others.

As you think of the different ways in which Jesus used the gift of encouragement and support, recall for a moment His disciples. There was the quiet one, Andrew. Jesus could see his potential even through his shyness. Peter was the opposite. He was outspoken, rough around the edges. Yet, Peter was supported even at the same time he was being chiseled and shaped. Jesus knew that Peter could be the "rock man," in the ministry of the early Church and in spreading the Word.

Take a look at Matthew. Because he collected taxes for Roman coffers, he and his profession were greatly despised. Often, in those days, the only way to earn a living wage was through some form of dishonesty. Matthew did very well for himself by overcharging people on their taxes. Yet this was the same man Jesus chose for one of the Twelve (see Mark 2:13-17; Luke 5:27-31).

Paul, the apostle, who wrote much of the New Testament, had formerly been a Pharisee. He had persecuted the Church of Jesus (see Phil. 3:5-6). Yet, he was miraculously transformed on the road to Damascus and then he was able to be used mightily for Jesus.

Jesus associated with different kinds of people. It did not matter whether they were man or woman, young or old, or even if they had failed over and over. He always encouraged them in their faith, their future and gave them renewed hope in their new tomorrows. In almost every incident you can see where Jesus used His gift of encouragement and support. Yet it is easier for us to notice His gifts of preaching, teaching and healing, as they were more pronounced. As a result, many of us have indeed overlooked His basic gift, which was encouragement and support. This gift was so vital and important in His ministry and He used it continually in magnificent ways as He minister to people. The genuine compassion He showed and expressed enhanced the growth of His believers.

Jesus spent a great amount of His time being with all types of people. The stories we read of Him eating, sitting around a fire, laughing, crying or just playing with children are throughout Scripture. These moments He had with others were of tremendous encouragement to them.

Can you imagine yourself personally sitting with Jesus and having Him laugh with you, talk with you? How very aware you would be of the total and complete love He had for you. What effect do you think that type of caring attitude would have on your life?

A BIBLICAL UNDERSTANDING OF SUPPORT

Throughout Scripture are many examples of how people encouraged one another. There are examples of how people were stretcher-bearers in both the Old and the New Testaments.

In 1 Samuel 18, we read the story of Jonathan and David, of their special friendship and of the way in which they encouraged and supported one another. In Exodus 17, we read of Aaron and Hur and of how they held up the arms of Moses in the defeat of the Amalakites. These two men allowed themselves to be used to support Moses at a critical time in his life.

In the New Testament, Paul encouraged a young minister named Timothy. Where would Timothy have been without the encouragement and support he received through the letters Paul wrote to him? Galatians 6:2 (*KJV*) says, "Bear ye one another's burdens, and so fulfill the law of Christ." Also found in the New Testament is the evidence of support and encouragement the Apostle Peter gave to the young disciple, Mark (see 1 Pet. 5:13).

But, what about Jesus? Was the gift of encouragement and support also vital for Him, for His ministry and for His well-being? We have read how, when Jesus went to the Garden of Gethsemane, He did not want to go alone, but wanted to be supported by three special friends, Peter, James and John (see

Mark 14:33). Here is a classic example of our Lord desiring support and encouragement in His own life.

The Lord's disciple John was a special friend and encourager to Jesus, a beloved disciple who had played a vital part in the support of Jesus (John 13:23; 20:2:21:7:20). This was especially evident when Jesus, though suffering on the cross, encouraged John to take care of His mother, Mary. John responded to Jesus as that special friend by caring for Mary as he would his own mother (John 19:25-27). He became a stretcher-bearer, a person of encouragement and support.

A SPECIAL FRIEND

As you can see, the gift of encouragement and support is throughout Scripture, the classic example being Proverbs 18:24: "A man of many companions may come to ruin, but there is a friend who sticks closer than a brother." *The Living Bible* puts it this way, "There are 'friends' who pretend to be friends, but there is a friend who sticks closer than a brother."

I have *two* questions that I would like to pose to you for your own consideration and growth.

My *first* question is this: If you had your Bible in front of you and you underlined Proverbs 18:24 with a pen, whose name would you write down in your Bible as your special friend? Take a moment to think about this right now. This question is so very important. In one of my Bibles I have written the name "Dave." Later on you will see how important Dave is to me as that "special friend."

My second question is this: Do you think anyone would write your name in his or her Bible? Yes or no? Answer this question as honestly as you can.

Spend some time now thinking deeply about both these questions.

Do we have that special friend, or are we that special friend to someone else? Are we really brother and sister to one another?

You see, Christianity is more than just going to church. Christianity is that intimate relationship with Him lived out among one another. It is being a stretcher-bearer. It is people encouraging and supporting one another in the name of Jesus Christ.

PERSONAL STRETCHER BEARERS

The basic principle that undergirds the entire concept of stretcher bearing is a simple one and is revealed by the answer to this question: What caused the miracle in the stretcher-bearing story of Mark 2? We find the answer in verse 5: "When Jesus saw their faith."

Whose faith? The words "their faith" refer to the faith of the four men who carried the stretcher. Jesus was moved when He saw the faith of these men. Yes, Jesus did the healing, but the miracle was made possible by the men bringing their friend into the presence of Jesus. They had faith and acted on it. Without their caring and support, the miracle might not have taken place.

THE STRETCHER WAITS

Another thought I want to share is that the stretcher is for all at one time or another. Each one of us will, at some time, be the man or woman on the stretcher. Now that might not be the best news you hear today, but friend, it's going to happen eventually. It could be something that will affect you either physically, mentally, socially or spiritually.

Someone may be hurting in some way in your family. This would then cause you to feel hurt too. All of us experience the death of someone dear. A husband or wife, a mom or dad, a grandma or grandpa. Any of these events can put us on a stretcher, and we will definitely feel the need of supportive people around us. Yes, indeed, there will be those moments in our lives where each one of us is that person on a stretcher.

WHEN STRETCHER TIMES HAPPEN

Stretcher times can, and do happen, when we least expect it. A few years ago I had the experience of being on that stretcher.

My wife, Gilda, and I had just experienced the birth of our first child. Having a child was a dream come true for us, and we were both overjoyed with our beautiful new daughter. Nicole. I had wanted a daughter through most of my wife's pregnancy, so I was really excited when it was time to bring my baby daughter home.

Everything was going great and I was 10 feet off the ground. It was summertime and I had just started vacation. My little daughter was growing every day, and when she was six weeks old I remember feeling that the Lord had given me everything I needed in life. I had a beautiful home, a good wife and a new baby daughter. I sensed that God had really blessed us. I was feeling very thankful.

Then one evening in August, I was watching the news when suddenly my wife screamed from our bedroom, "Mike, Mike, hurry up! Come here! Nicole isn't breathing!" I ran from the living room into the bedroom and picked up my tiny daughter! I held her up in front of me! Her eyes were open yet she wasn't breathing! She looked like a little Raggedy Ann doll, her head tilted to the side, so light – only eight or nine pounds. As I held her I felt she was dying in my arms!

I told Gilda to call the paramedics! She immediately ran into the kitchen and telephoned, and then rushed outside so she could wait for them. In the meantime, I began to try to stimulate my baby so she would start to breathe again. I yelled at her and screamed, "Nicole, Nicole, breathe!" I patted her hard on the back.

Nothing was working! Through my tears I looked up toward the Lord and prayed, "Don't let her die, Lord, please don't let her die. I love her Lord." With tears coming down my face, I kept yelling, "Nicole, Nicole, breathe...Nicole, Nicole." I continued to hit her hard on the back for what seemed an eternity.

Finally, I heard this little whimper and her first little breath. She then began to cry and continued to breathe. I was so grateful and relieved to be able to feel her little body respond and to know she was wonderfully alive. The paramedics came and checked her over and, to our relief, assured us that she now appeared to be doing fine. However, one paramedic advised us to go see our doctor in the morning.

The next day we did go to see her pediatrician and he admitted Nicole to Children's Hospital in Los Angeles. It's a marvelous hospital, but it is sad to go to a hospital that just deals with children and their illnesses. It is very hard to see so many children sick or in pain. There is so much you want to do and you feel very inadequate in being unable to relieve their individual hurts. However, we were thankful to be there with Nicole and to see the care she received. They gave Nicole quite a variety of tests so they could best diagnose and evaluate her problem.

After five days of these tests, we had the results. The specialist, Dr. Keens, called Gilda and me into his office and said, "The tests are finalized and your daughter has what is called, 'crib death,' meaning 'Sudden Infant Death Syndrome." This means she runs an extremely high risk of having her breathing suddenly stop, and she could die."

I could not believe what I had just heard. My wife and I returned to our hotel room to gather our thoughts. As soon as I sat on the bed, I began to cry like a baby. I know I am supposed to be the spiritual leader of the home, but right then, it just hurt too much.

I felt I needed someone to support and encourage me at that moment. Just the presence of a friend would have been of comfort, as the care of Jesus can be so evident through others radiating His presence. Someone once said, "We are not called to be the Messiah, but the Messiah's servant."

Just six weeks earlier I was on top of the world. I finally had a child. Now suddenly, unexpectedly, I am not only on the stretcher, but my wife and my child are there with me! Who would have thought six weeks earlier that I would be at Children's Hospital, receiving such frightening news?

I then picked up the phone and called my parents. I shared with them the news of their granddaughter, that Nicole had Sudden Infant Death Syndrome, that she could quit breathing at any time.

Then suddenly it happened again. My eyes turned into faucets, and the tears poured out. Aware of my grief, Dad simply said, "Mom and I are on our way down." Our needed stretcher-bearers and the presence of God through others would now enter the world my wife and I were part of.

Gilda and I today have a real sense of thankfulness, relief and joy as we see our healthy, lively, growing daughter who brings such happiness into everyday living. But, we still remember that hard time and can vividly recall all that we experienced.

When we least expect it, you and I can be put on a stretcher. When we least expect it the stretcher time can come. When these times do come they hurt, and at that moment we need stretcher-bearers.

WHAT DESTROYS PEOPLE

Yes, all of us are going to experience good and bad times. But people are not necessarily destroyed or disheartened just because they find themselves, during one of those bad times, on a stretcher. What can destroy people, and often with suicidal results, is when people find themselves on stretchers and they feel no one cares. Or often there is no one there to carry their stretcher. Someone can then become so shattered that he or she gives up on faith, gives up on God and gives up on life.

Let me share with you the words of an actual suicide note. I share this to stress how important it is to show others that we care about their problems.

"Life isn't worth living. No one cares for me. No one will care if I live or die. Because of this I choose to die." I was saddened even more when I learned that the man who wrote this note had been a Christian. What destroyed him was not only being on a stretcher, but also feeling that no one could or would carry his stretcher and help him through his very troubled time.

I am firmly convinced that when you have no one to carry your stretcher, you are on dangerous ground.

LET'S THINK

Following these next two paragraphs is a picture of a stretcher. Write your own name in the middle of the stretcher. Now, think. Are there four people who would carry you, if you were physically, mentally, spiritually, socially or emotionally on a stretcher? Can you think of four people who would lift your stretcher? If so, fill in their names.

Do you have four people who would carry your stretcher? No? What about three or two or even one? I honestly would be saddened if you could not think of four people to carry your stretcher.

1. _____   2. _____

3. _____   4. _____

If you were able to identify four people, I encourage you now to get in touch with these people. Follow through today and let them know you believe in them as stretcher-bearers. Do this either by letter or phone. Let them know what it means to be encouraged and supported by people like them. Tell them what you have been reading here. And say that as you read it, you were asked to think of someone to carry your stretcher and when you did, you thought of him or her.

Can you imagine the bond that can be developed? When you reach out and tell someone you know that he or she is a person you feel cares about you, relationships are strengthened.

If you could put only one person's name on your list, don't feel badly. Perhaps this is a concept of the Christian faith that God, through His Spirit, is trying to teach you. As you continue to read about and understand the stretcher-bearer theme, God will bring those special people into your life. Then you in turn can become a stretcher-bearer to someone else.

I firmly believe that this concept of stretcher-bearers will benefit you and is needed in your life to strengthen your walk with God.

CLOSING THOUGHTS

I am convinced that being on a stretcher is not what destroys people. Rather, it is being on the stretcher and believing no one cares. That is what is so disheartening to so many.

In life we are all going to face those hard times, those issues that will place us upon a stretcher. We need to affirm and open ourselves to those stretcher-bearers in our life who can support and encourage us through stretcher times.

We all need to learn how to reach out and become stretcher-bearers to others. We must allow God to use us to encourage others when they are dealing with stretcher experiences. To be a stretcher bearer, using the gift of encouragement and support in another's life, is a powerful, personal ministry blessed by our Lord.

PERSONAL TIME

List the names of three friends. What have you contributed to each friendship and what have your friends contributed?

MY CONTRIBUTIONS

1. _____

_____

2. _____

_____

3. _____

_____

MY FRIEND'S CONTRIBUTIONS

1. _____

_____

2. _____

_____

3. _____

_____

GRAB A HANDLE

I encourage you to make contact with the friends you have listed and to verbally express your feelings about them and what they mean to you as a stretcher-bearer.

Note
*Seven outstanding gifts Jesus used in His ministry:
1. *Teaching*   5. *Faith*
2. *Encouragement and support*   6. *Discernment*
3. *Healing*   7. *Evangelism*
4. *Prophecy*

Jesus' most outstanding gift: *the gift of encouragement and support.* I did not attempt to list these gifts in their order of importance. Your own list of gifts might differ from mine, and your choices are probably just as valid.

THREE

HELP I'M DROWNING

As Christians, we have a new life in Christ. His life within us is not to be separate from our relationships with one another. On the contrary, we are called to support these relationships in a new and better way. We need other people and we are meant to encourage one another.

Every day we face difficulties and problems that require solutions. Some situations are harder than others, but life calls us to resolve them on a daily basis.

Not all of life's challenges, however, are of the everyday variety. Some are so severe that they literally place people on stretchers. Undoubtedly, some of these people will have others – stretcher-bearers – ready to reach out and help them. Yet many of these needy people will refuse the help of a stretcher-bearer. Why is it that many hurting people will not accept help from others? Let's examine the reasons behind such refusals.

NO CRY FOR HELP

I remember an incident that took place a few years ago at Huntington Beach. The summer day was beautiful, the sun was warm and it felt good to be down by the ocean. I walked into the water to do a little bodysurfing.

After riding a few waves, I began to swim back toward shore when I noticed something unusual about another swimmer. He was a young man, about 13 years of age and he was maybe 25 yards in front of me. He was struggling and as I watched him, I knew something was wrong! I quickly swam over to him, grabbed him and towed him back to the beach were we were both out of danger.

Bringing him to safety had proved to be no easy task, and afterwards we both sat on the sand for a while, exhausted. In a few moments I introduced myself, and he told me his name was Steve.

When we finally caught our breath I asked him a questions, "Steve, were you drowning out there?"

He bent his head and looked down at the sand. He hesitated and then answered, "Yes." Even though we had come through this experience together, this young man felt so embarrassed that he could not even look at me one-on-one. He could not look me in the eye!

After a moment I asked him a second question. "Steve, since you felt you were drowning, why didn't you cry out for help?"

Almost immediately he turned, looked at me and said, "Cry out for help, Mike? What would my friends think if I cried out for help?'

I sat there stunned. I could not believe what I had heard! *How foolish.* I thought. In another minute, Steve would have drowned. Yet, no matter what, he would not have cried out for help! He was going to make it on his own or not make it at all.

This incident left me realizing that here is an issue people must learn to deal with. Why is it so many people refuse to reach out for help? No doubt you know people right now who are going through great difficulties in their lives and are probably on stretchers. Is one reading this book?

Why is it, like that young man at Huntington Beach, so many people find it difficult to say, "Help, I need you! I need encouragement. I need support. I don't think I can do it alone?" Why do people refuse to reach out for help and support? Why do we find it hard to admit we need encouragement?

In Mark 9:17-24, we read about a certain father who has been suffering tremendous emotional pain and is on a stretcher. The reason he is on a stretcher is because he loves his son, and the boy is sick. Now that sickness has not only affected the child, but because of the father's love for him, it has also affected the father as well. Read the story for yourself.

> A man in the crowd answered, "Teacher, I brought you my only son, who is possessed by a spirit that has robbed him of speech. Whenever it seizes him, it throws him to the ground. He foams at the mouth, gnashes his teeth and becomes rigid. I asked your disciples to drive out the spirit, but they could not."

> "O unbelieving generation," Jesus replied, "How long shall I stay with you? How long shall I put up with you? Bring the boy to me."

> So they brought him. When the spirit saw Jesus, it immediately threw the boy into a convulsion. He fell to the ground and rolled around, foaming at the mouth.

> Jesus asked the boy's father, "How long has he been like this?"

> "From childhood," he answered. "It has often thrown him into fire or water to kill him. But if you can do anything, take pity on us and help us."

> "'If you can?'" said Jesus. "Everything is possible for him who believes."

> Immediately the boy's father exclaimed, "I do believe; help me overcome my unbelief!"

Let's take another look at the father in this story and study him closely. From what he does, we will be able to learn some valuable lessons. These lessons can keep us from having to drown. We can also learn why people refuse to reach out for help. Even though we may learn how to ask for help, many of us will still do just the opposite of what we learn.

WHY NO CRY FOR HELP?

I want to give you four reasons why I believe people are on stretchers and refusing the aid of stretcher-bearers; why they are almost fearful of reaching out for help.

The Fear of Being Authentic and Honest

First of all, refusing to ask for or accept help has to do with the fear of being authentic and honest. We walk around with our masks on, parading past one another. The smiles are there, even a calmness about us, but what are we feeling inside? Who are we as people? Are we inwardly saying, "Do I dare take my mask off and become real? Can I be authentic and honest about my feelings and about who I am as a person?"

I believe wonderful relationships develop when we let our masks fall and become real. If we can admit who we really are, I believe this will allow God to place people within our lives who will accept us, and we will be bonded closer to them through the experience.

A very important man in my life who has taught me what it means to be real, authentic and honest is my father.

In 1969, I was drafted into the United States Army to go overseas and fight in the Viet Nam War. The morning I was to leave to board a jet for Seattle, an incident took place that will forever be with me.

My father and I went to the airport alone. Mother did not feel she could go through the experience of seeing me leave, so she did not go with us.

The drive from our house in Glendale, California, to Los Angeles International Airport is about 45 minutes. During the drive my father did not say one word to me. He drove while I quietly looked out the window. I remember thinking about certain landmarks that perhaps I would never see again.

We arrived and went to the United Airlines counter. I received my boarding pass and proceeded with my dad to gate number 14 where the jet for Seattle was waiting. I was to be in Seattle for three days of processing before going on to Viet Nam.

At the gate, we walked over to those big windows airports provide for people to look out and see the planes coming and going. We stood there and observed the 727 jet I would soon be flying on that day, knowing that in a few minutes it would take me on to Seattle.

Our silence was interrupted by a message coming over the intercom, "Flight 107 for Seattle is now ready to board." At this moment, Dad spoke for the first time. "You have time to board, they will call you at least two more times. You don't have to leave yet."

Dad, however, continued to look straight ahead and out through the window as he spoke. I turned to look at him for a moment and I saw something I will never forget. Running from his eyes and over his cheeks were tears. Dad was crying.

Suddenly again over the intercom came that same message: "Flight 107 for Seattle is now boarding."

Again, Dad responded by saying, "They'll call a third." So we stood there, father and son, for yet another minute.

Then the third message came: "This is the final boarding call for flight 107 for Seattle."

It was then that Dad did turn to look at me. And for the first time he really spoke. "Son, I love you and I'm going to miss you and right now I'm hurting as a father because I don't want to see you go. One day you will be a father and know how a moment like this will hurt. I love you Michael." He reached out, hugged me, gave me a kiss and said, "I'll see you again, and I'll be praying for you."

I boarded that jet with tears in my own eyes, and for the whole flight to Seattle, I did not say one word to anyone. All I could do was think of my father's face, his tears and what he had said to me.

Now some might think that at this particular time in our lives, perhaps my dad should have been stronger. After all, I was the one going to war, not he. At this time, wouldn't I have needed a strong dad who could look at me and say, "Son, it's going to be all right. Trust in God. We're behind you and don't worry. You're going to make it back?"

But Dad had not been able to say that because he was on a stretcher and he had risked himself by being open and honest. He allowed me to share in his own hurt even as he continued to share in mine. That exchange of honest love and caring created a wonderful bond between my father and me. Words are inadequate to describe its strength even to this day.

Yes, my dad was really on a stretcher at that moment. He was drowning in his own sorrow and hurt. Yet, he did risk himself by letting his mask fall and allowing himself to be an authentic and honest father to me.

Wonderful relationships do develop between people when they let their true feelings become known. Unfortunately, many of us will still allow ourselves to drown. We will lie on our stretchers alone because we cannot reveal our true selves by being honest with one another.

Now, what of the father in Mark 9? Was this father a real, authentic, honest man? Did he speak honestly to the Lord about his feelings, about his faith, about his hurts and about his child? Did he hide behind a mask or did he let himself be known?

From the Scripture, we see that this father was open, and by laying himself before Jesus in his own need, he allowed Jesus to lift up his stretcher.

The Fear of Rejection and Nonacceptance

Even though people often have the basic desire to share their needs, many are fearful of being authentic and honest. Why? They become afraid because of the fear of rejection and nonacceptance. This fear of rejection and nonacceptance is the second most important reason many people have drowned or are drowning, while others are lying on their stretchers today, just waiting their turn to drown.

Do I dare to risk myself with you by dropping my mask? Do I dare to share my victories and struggles? Or, do I become less in your eyes if you don't see me as a spiritual giant and as a man who has everything together in his Christian walk?

For instance, when the doctor told my wife and me about the strong possibility that our baby could die at any moment, I then returned to the hotel room, called my parents on the phone and told them the news. I share with you again the fact that I cried like a baby as I did so. Faucets turned on in my eyes and the tears would not stop falling.

Even though I was hurting that much at the time, I still recognized I was supposed to be the spiritual giant and leader of my family. But right then I had no strength of my own to lead. Does sharing such personal knowledge of myself make me somehow less in your eyes?

Lisa, a young married woman in my church, spent nearly two months of her pregnancy in the hospital. She lost nearly 20 pounds of weight as her baby developed within her. She was so sick to her stomach that it was impossible for her to eat and keep any food down.

I spent a great amount of time visiting with Lisa in the hospital, praying with her, talking to her, trying to lend her support and encouragement. One afternoon in particular, I looked her directly in the eyes and said, "Lisa, have you ever felt that our prayers were just bouncing off the ceiling?"

She looked at me and without hesitation said, "Yes."

I asked her, "Lisa, are you as frustrated as I am?"

Once again, with a little smile, she said, "Yes, I am." I went on to say, "But we can't just give up, Lisa, even if it feels like we could put on a tape recording with our prayer repeating itself, over and over. We can't give up! We have to continue to come to God with these real feelings we have as people."

These honest statements that had been said to Lisa; did they draw us closer together or farther apart? It's important to realize we were definitely drawn closer together through this experience. We became real people, supporting one another. I was being a truly honest pastor who was dealing with a frustrating, hurtful issue.

I, with many friends and members of her family were supportive of Lisa, and her husband Keith, throughout this difficult pregnancy. I was there at the hospital when that precious child was born, and later had the privilege of dedicating him to the Lord while his parents held him in their arms and other family members stood around them in support. Today, this child is walking, talking and is full of life and energy. I believe God used this whole incident to draw all of us even closer to one another.

At this difficult time in Lisa and Keith's lives, they were on a stretcher and each one of us dared not only to be honest and open, but we also dared to risk ourselves despite the fear of rejection and nonacceptance.

Yes, many of us refuse to admit that we are on any kind of a stretcher because we fear rejection. The drowning boy, Steve, would not cry out for help. His reason? "What would my friends think?" Steve had said. He knew at that moment of danger he was weak and not the strongest man in the world. But, he thought if he opened himself up and admitted his need, his friends would not accept him for who he was.

Look again at the father in Mark 9. Had he risked rejection and nonacceptance by Jesus? Of course, he had! He spoke openly of himself; even admitting his faith was not as strong as it should be. His words really said that, because of the hardship and duration of his son's illness, the hurt for his child was overtaking even his faith.

He shared these things about himself with the Lord, not knowing whether Jesus would accept or reject him. The boy's father risked rejection. And the Lord not only accepted him in his honesty and openness, but He also had compassion on him and his son, and He healed the boy.

The Foolishness of Pride

The third reason many of us allow ourselves to be left alone to drown without help is our pride. Proverbs 16:18 warns, "Pride goes before destruction."

Many willing people are rowing around in sturdy lifeboats. They are calling out supportive words such as, "Let us help you into this boat." Yet the words fall upon deaf ears. You see, many people are ready and willing to lift the stretcher of someone in need, yet the response from that someone is often, "No thank you. I can do it on my own."

How many times have you heard someone make that statement? What about yourself? When was the last time you said those same words? I am convinced this is a foolish statement of pride.

Now pride can be healthy to a point, if you see that pride as self-belief or self-worth and it adds a measure of encouragement into your life. I think we all need to feel that type of pride within ourselves. We need to feel that we are important, that we have capabilities, gifts and talents and that what God has freely given us that we can use to help make our lives happy and successful today.

However, pride can also be detrimental. If we turn on the burner of pride to full force, we burn out almost everything else around us. Our egos take over, our heads begin to swell to twice their normal size, and we begin to see ourselves on a throne saying, "I don't need anyone. I can do it alone, I can do it by myself." We then may find that what was once self-worth and self-belief has ultimately become egotistical self-destruction.

Pride is something that we all seem to have plenty of. We need not to be fearful of trampling on it or destroying it, for pride always grows back very quickly. There is something within our human systems that allows pride to spring up and return constantly throughout our lives.

We must learn to let pride work for us not against us. Once again, I refer to the father in the story of Mark 9. We see him as a humble, down-to-earth sort of man, not as a man of pride who says he can deal with this issue by himself because he is a strong father! On the contrary, we see a man coming before God saying, "This is what I am, and at this moment I need you to work through me."

The Guilt of Faithlessness

Let's look now at the most honest statement of Mark 9. It shows us one of the main reasons why people refuse help. An interesting thing about this reason is that it is probably the number one Christian hang-up. What is it? It is the guilt of faithlessness.

> Jesus asked the boy's father, "How long has he been like this?"

"From childhood," he answered. "It has often thrown him into fire or water to kill him. But if you can do anything, take pity on us and help us." "'If you can?'" said Jesus. "Everything is possible for him who believes." Immediately the boy's father exclaimed, "I do believe; help me overcome my unbelief!" (9:21-24)

Verse 24 bears witness to one of the most honest statements said by anyone in the Bible. The father said to Jesus, "I do believe, help me overcome my unbelief." He was sharing with the Lord that he had faith. He had faith or he would not have deliberately put himself in the presence of Jesus. Yet the stretcher that he was on, because of his son, was affecting his faith. This was hurting him to such a degree that, yes, his faith had diminished a little – yet it was not dead.

A result of recognized diminished faith can be a feeling of guilt. Therefore, the father could have wrapped himself in the guilt and thought how in the world could I come before Jesus when my faith is not as strong as it should be? How can I possibly come before Jesus when this stretcher situation is so unbearable that it is affecting my relationship with God? Yet he came to God, with the faith he had. Even though it was not as strong as it should have been, he still offered what he had to God, overcoming and surpassing any guilty feelings.

Many of us today do understand and respond, and yet we think in a totally different way from this certain father. We find ourselves perhaps thinking that if it's true that I need help, then I need prayer and I need support, but what does that really say about my personal relationship with God? Will my friends respond to me by saying, "Don't you trust God? Don't you have faith in God?"

Today, many Christians refuse to reach out for help because they surround themselves with feelings of guilt concerning their degree of faith. We as Christians are taught to believe that we should never sway and never feel less than mighty if we are truly walking close with Jesus Christ. If we should reach out for help, does this perhaps mean that we are not trusting in God and leaning upon His strength?

Through this story of Mark 9, we see a father who is completely real and who allows himself the freedom from having the guilt of faithlessness. He had explained to Jesus with all the honesty he had that his son was really suffering. Then he became very vulnerable when he asked, "Can you do anything?"

"'If you can?'" said Jesus. Everything is possible for him who believes."

Pause for a moment and think about that statement Jesus made. What was going through the mind of the father? What about the times in your life when faith seems to be diminishing? How would you respond? How do you think Jesus would want you to respond?

Visualize this father as he is trying to express himself. Perhaps his feelings were saying, "But Lord, the part of me that is hurting right now, it hinders me and I can't totally believe as I should. Yet, I believe in you Lord, or I wouldn't be here. But right now I am hurting so much for my son. I believe in you, please help me overcome my unbelief and accept me for who I am."

Jesus does respond to the father's request and He heals the son of his illness.

THOUGHT QUESTIONS

In this chapter you have had a glimpse into the lives of two different men. One is the father in mark 9 and the other is Steve, the young man from Huntington Beach. Both were on stretchers and each responded differently.

I gave you four reasons why people allow themselves to drown. Perhaps you are able to think of even more. I believe, however, that the four reasons given, the fear of being real and honest, the fear of rejection and nonacceptance, the foolishness of pride and the guilt of faithlessness are the major ones.

Now I want to ask you some honest questions. First, which of the four reasons concerns you personally? Are any of those four reasons a weight around your own neck that, in effect, could cause you to drown? If Steve were here today I think he would say that the fear of rejection and nonacceptance was the weight that almost took his life. Which one is it for you? Which one does God want you to be released from?

Another question I have for you is, why is the guilt of faithlessness such a hang-up for Christians? Why do we feel that our love and devotion to God is tarnished because of those times we just don't feel as strong? What have you been taught? How do you deal with the situations and the stretcher times that honestly affect your faith?

My last question is: Are you on a stretcher with no help from anyone? Can you honestly say to yourself that maybe the issue is not the people around you? Maybe there are many people who really want to help you and who want to lift your stretcher! Maybe the issue is that you refuse to reach out for help and support and have found it hard to admit that you need encouragement.

Pray honestly and openly that the Lord will show you why you and others are drowning. Ask Him to help you recognize and accept the help from your own personal stretcher-bearers who are reaching out to you.

PERSONAL TIME

A. Think of people you know on stretchers who refuse help. Take time to identify the issues that keep them from seeking help. List ways in which you can provide trust.

Friends and Issue	*How I Can Build Trust*
1. _____	1. _____
_____	_____
2. _____	2. _____
_____	_____
3. _____	3. _____
_____	_____

B. What are the issues that hinder you from reaching out? List corrections you could make.

My Issues	*How I Can Build Trust*
1. _____	1. _____
_____	_____
2. _____	2. _____
_____	_____
3. _____	3. _____
_____	_____

GRAB A HANDLE

Close in silent prayer on behalf of someone you think might be drowning. Ask God to open the door for you regarding ministering and helping this person. God bless you as you minister.

FOUR
OFF THE SHORE, INTO THE WATER!

"How can people be like that? How can people see someone in need and not respond?" The lady speaking to me was visibly angry. Her voice, her facial expressions left no doubt about their feelings. She was looking directly into my eyes, and I could see how outraged and upset she was.

At the time of our encounter, I was at a conference, speaking on the ministry of encouragement and support. During a break in the program, this lady, Betty, had asked if she could have a few moments of my time. She wanted to tell me about a recent happening that had truly disturbed her. We sat down over a cup of coffee.

WHEN THE CRY FOR HELP COMES
A True Story

Betty told me about the lake just outside her city where, in the summertime, many people gather, picnicking, swimming and generally enjoying themselves. One day a young boy swimming in the lake met with some difficulty. No one knew if he had developed a cramp or not. But everyone present knew that, far out there in that lake, the boy was calling for help.

Yet no one responded. His cries soon turned to screams. Still, not a single person moved. Then, after a few moments, no more cries or screams were heard. The boy had slipped beneath the surface, and only silence remained where he had disappeared from view. He had drowned because no one had even tried to help him.

Betty's question continued to hang in the air over us: How can people see someone in need and not respond?

As Betty ended her shocking story, I paused for a minute to collect my thoughts. I really wanted to answer Betty's question, but how should I reply? What could I say that would be adequate? How could other people simply not respond to a drowning boy's cries for help? Finally, in reply, I told her the following story that also takes place at a lake.

A Modern-day Parable

Picture the setting. The lake is surrounded by a beautiful shoreline. On the shore are two separate groups of people. The people in one group are Christians; those in the other group are non-Christians.

Everyone is enjoying himself on this warm summer day. Then a young boy decides to go in for a swim, but he soon finds himself in real trouble. He starts crying out for help.

The non-Christians on the shore carry on as though nothing is happening. But the people from the Christian group notice the drowning boy and quickly respond with encouraging words:

"Hang in there!"

"Don't give up!"

"We're praying for you!"

"Help's coming!"

The Christians also start yelling to the other group, "Come on, you guys. This boy needs help. Don't just sit there."

Then suddenly everyone notices the silence. The young boy's cries aren't heard anymore. He has disappeared beneath the surface of the water.

Word of mouth quickly spreads the shocking news of the boy's death. Newspaper reporters and radio and television crews rush to the scene and begin interviewing eyewitnesses:

"What happened here today?"

"Were you on the beach at the time and can you tell us what you saw?"

A few people attempt to tell what they think happened. A reporter suddenly interrupts everyone and asks, "But is there anyone here who actually responded to the boy's cries for help?"

The Christian group turns noticeably defensive as someone answers, "Yes – we did. We told the boy not to give up. We said that help was on the way. At least we're not like that other group of people over there," referring to the non-Christians. "They hardly said a word."

The reporter persists and now asks, "But who got wet? Who actually went into the water?"

The television crew slowly pans the crowded shore with their camera. Apparent to all is the fact that no one looks even slightly wet. All are dry, making it evident that no one actually went into the water. No one got wet trying to rescue that young boy in need of someone's help.

Why No Answer To The Cry For Help?

As I continued talking to Betty I drew a parallel between the Christian people in my story and our Christian churches today. Unfortunately, too often when individual Christians are drowning in needs, their churches are back on the shore, only reciting "encouraging" words they have committed to memory. It's fine to say, "I'll pray for you," to hurting people, but not when it is said in place of reaching out realistically and practically to help hurting humanity. Again and again, the key question, "So who's getting wet?" unfortunately remains unanswered.

Much of humanity today seems to be drowning in whole lakes of misery and distress. So the need is great today for people to encourage and support one another with actual physical help. Why then do so many who could help simply stay on the shore? Why is it difficult for them to go into the water where the hurting people are? As I searched for answers I began thinking of all the reasons or excuses we use in refusing to get involved in the hurts of others.

We Are Too Self-Centered

If a person is self-centered, how big a part does such a preoccupation play in our lack of response to the needs and concerns of others? One day, I heard a popular song that caught my attention. The song is secular, but in it were some lines that captured my mind. The message of the song stayed with me because it was about an individual wanting our world to be a better place than it is and wondering how to make it happen.

As he thinks about a changed world, he gradually realizes that, if he really wants that change made, he'd better take a hard look at himself. Why? Because no change will take place unless he helps to make it happen.

Any change then that he wants made will have to start with him. And that's when he recognizes that, as he talks about making changes – he really has been talking to the man in his own mirror – himself. That makes him admit, in the second verse of the song, that he has been victimized by a selfish kind of love.

So what are these lyrics saying to me? They were saying that if I want to bring change into this world, I must do something myself to bring about that change. It won't just happen. So I need to take a good look into my own mirror and have a serious talk with the person I see there. Because otherwise, all I see reflected in my mirror are myself, my own concerns, my own needs, my own well being. My self-centeredness, the personal *I* is what will keep me from venturing into the water to rescue someone else.

Are you a "victim" of "a selfish kind of love?" Without having realized it before, perhaps you are. If so, being engrossed in yourself will keep you and others like you from ever venturing from the shore. Self-centeredness has the power to keep you from caring enough about other people to ever reach out and help them. Ask yourself, "Am I a victim of a selfish kind of love?"

We Are Too Apathetic

"Apathy" is a word of Greek origin that means "without emotion." The word itself sounds somewhat pathetic and unfeeling. If you accused someone of apathy, that person would probably bristle and say, "Who? Not me!"

Do you find "complacency" or "indifference" more comfortable words than "apathy?" No matter, choose whichever word you feel best describes the condition spoken of by John in Revelation 3:16: "So, because you are lukewarm – neither hot nor cold – I am about to spit you out of my mouth."

One day as some college students sat in their classroom, their professor wrote the word "apathy" on the chalkboard. One young man, after looking at the word, turned to a classmate and asked, "Apathy – what does that mean?"

His friend responded, "I don't know and I don't really care."

To me, apathy explains the reasons many people give for not getting involved in rescuing a hurting world. I define apathy as "the numbing of America." With apathy going through your system like Novocaine, you're numb. You are oblivious to any hurt or pain surrounding you.

Apathy explains why a great many individuals, if asked to help people in need, typically respond, "I need to think about it." "If I find I have the time," "If I can get around to it" or even "I need to pray about it before thinking of getting involved." Then time, as always, moves swiftly ahead, and those individuals wind up doing nothing. There they are, still sitting on the shore, while those in need go down for the last time.

The fact that I became a pastor – a man of God – didn't just happen without people caring for me. Looking at who and what I am today makes me thankful, as I realize how fortunate I have been. Three special people have made a definite difference in my life. They are Chuck Davis and a married couple, Bruce and Sue Caldwell.

When I was in third grade, Chuck was my Sunday School teacher. Then when I was older in our church's college group, the Caldwell's were our sponsors. These three wonderful individuals took the time to care about people. Because they were willing to get involved, they made a difference in many lives. And they made that difference; because when they saw a need they always responded and met it.

Now, what about you? Are you making a difference in someone's life? Are you involved in any kind of ministry? Have you ventured off the shore and into the water?

Remember, apathy makes a person want only to sit. Such an individual has no desire even to get wet, much less learn how to swim.

We Are Afraid of Risk

The word "risk" means different things to different people. One person thinks of risk only in a financial sense. Someone else will think of risk in a physical sense where bodily harm is possible.

Looking at risk in another way, it can mean getting yourself involved in another person's life, particularly when you want to feel the situation is really none of your business – but your conscience tells you otherwise. Risking yourself usually makes you stop first, think about any negative considerations, weigh the odds involved and then try to make a decision. Just this thinking process takes time and can itself cause you to remain on shore instead of taking the plunge.

What happens that holds you back? You have recognized that risking is dangerous, and you naturally want to avoid taking a risk. After all, if you venture into water that is hazardous, you could very well be caught and swept away by a swift current. Even when the water is still, if it is extremely cold, the near-freezing temperature alone can be life threatening. Besides that, who wants to take an ice-cold plunge anyway? Of course you don't.

But neither can you wait for spa-like conditions before getting off the shore and into the water, because there are just too many people out there today who are cold, alone and in great distress, and the tremendous currents of life are not going to stop. So if you wait for those ideal conditions before getting wet, someone you know will simply go under.

In January 1982, during a heavy snowstorm, a Florida-bound Boeing 737 went down in Washington, DC almost immediately after takeoff from Dulles International Airport. Investigators later determined that, as the plane sat on an airport runway awaiting flight clearance, excessive snow and ice built up on the wings. Then when the flight crew tried to take off, the overburdened plane was unable to gain enough lift and airspeed to stay aloft.

An instant of shocked silence followed the crash, and then people began running everywhere. In the distance, barely audible, sirens began sounding. People started gathering along the shoreline below the bridge, while others still on the bridge stared down at the scene below. But all anyone could see were a few survivors surfacing from the plane and struggling to stay afloat by clinging to the wreckage.

Some of the spectators called to those in the water, yelling, "Come on, don't give up!" "You can make it to shore, come on!" But out of the many gathered around on the riverbanks that fateful day, only one person actually dove into that ice-choked water to offer physical help. Just one person. All offered words, but only one offered rescue.

What can we learn from this terrible tragedy that enables us to focus better on how we can help one another? Shouldn't we Christians, as the loving, caring people we claim to be, stop our yelling and shouting from the shore and start risking getting wet? If not, how else are we going to meet the needs and heal the hurts of those around us?

We Are Short of Time

Time – or the seeming lack of it – is another factor, which causes us to hold back from responding to other people in need. We simply resent the time it takes to venture out into the water. Consequently, we easily convince ourselves that we simply do not have enough time to help, or get involved. Surrendering personal time for the sake of someone else is apparently too costly a price for many Christians to pay.

At a conference on the Ministry of Encouragement and Support, I asked a group of 66 people what factor would be the most costly for them to overcome to be an encourager or stretcher bearer. When they had finished writing down their thoughts, I asked how many had written down the word "time." Fifty-five people from this group of 66 raised their hands. In response, I said to them, "I hate to be the bearer of bad news, but guess what? Nobody here is going to get any more time. Individually or together, we all have the same 24 hours in each day, no more – no less."

Yes, time is a precious commodity. It is always in short supply. You always need more time, it seems, but how do you find more time? How do you find the time necessary to reach out to an aching world, yet do so within the total amount of time available to you for all you need to do?

A family within our church congregation is an example of those who have found the time to be stretcher-bearers. The parents and their three children are not only involved within the church, but also in the outside community as well. I have observed this family ministering to and caring for others. I stand in utter amazement of all they are able to do.

A study of their life-style reveals they have the same demands on their time that the rest of us face. They encounter the same long hours and pressures at work, along with raising growing kids, tackling yard work and dealing with all the other everyday issues that surround all of us in this fast-paced world. Yet there they are, month after month, quietly ministering to people. Sometimes, as I observe all they are able to do, I feel a sense of shame. And I often want to ask them that important question. But, where do you get the time?

Do you know where they get the time to minister so readily to others? You may not see it as first, but I believe Matthew 14:25-32 gives us the answer. And the answer is not only for this family, but for each one of us as well.

"During the fourth watch of the night" – which was about 3:00 in the morning – "Jesus went out to them, walking on the lake" (vs. 25). Picture yourself in the situation of the disciples. There you are out there on the water in the midst of the storm. And suddenly coming toward you out of the night is a figure – and it's walking on the water! Imagine what your reactions would be.

"When the disciples saw him walking on the lake, they were terrified. 'It's a ghost,' they said, and cried out in fear.

"But Jesus immediately said to them: 'Take courage! It is I. Don't be afraid.'

"'Lord, if it's you,' Peter replied, 'tell me to come to you on the water.'

"'Come,' he said" (vvs. 6-29).

Well, Peter instantly did what Jesus said. He got out of that boat. And he was walking on the water!

But then he noticed the wind (vs. 30). It was then "he was afraid and, beginning to sink, cried out, 'Lord, save me!'"

Then Jesus did what? "Immediately Jesus reached out his hand and caught him. 'You of little faith,' he said, 'why did you doubt?'" (vs. 31).

Do you see now why this family in our church was able to leave the shore and go into the water where the hurting people are? Not yet? I believe they are able to go into the water for the same reason Peter was able to walk on the water – because their eyes are on Jesus. Yes, when your eyes are focused upon the Master, your perspective on everything, including the use of time, changes. You think differently, you see differently and you act differently.

When your eyes are steadfastly focused on Jesus Christ, you realize that giving your life to Him is more than just going to church. It's allowing Him to grip you, to mold you and to influence your life in such a loving way that you are motivated into giving back that love in full measure to others. You are then able to do as Jesus commanded, to "love your neighbor as yourself." (Matt. 19:19; 22:39). When others and their needs become that important to you, personal considerations become secondary, and that includes concern over the time it takes to rescue others who are drowning in hurt and despair.

As Jesus shows you how to put everything into perspective, all those obstacles preventing you from getting off the shore and into the water will fall away. Self-centeredness is replaced with a love for others; apathy turns into enthusiasm; the fear of taking risks becomes a desire to get involved; and not having enough time gives way to letting the Lord replace personal priorities with His own.

And where will the strength come from you to be and do all this? Your strength will not come from yourself; the source of strength enabling you to be a stretcher-bearer will be Jesus Himself. "I can do everything through him who gives me strength" (Phil. 4:13). You can make that declaration today with the same assurance that Paul did when he wrote those words to the Philippians. Just keep your eyes on the Lord.

FAITH AND POWER TO ANSWER THE CRY FOR HELP

When your eyes are focused on Jesus Christ, you awaken to the fact that faith and trust in Him makes you want to be involved in some kind of ministry. That desire to get involved enables you to get off that shore you've been sitting on and go straight into the water to help in any way you can. For it's in that water where real ministry takes place.

Seeing Jesus walk upon the water had an immediate impact upon Peter. So when Jesus invited him to do the same, faith and trust caused Peter to respond immediately. And in faith, Peter also walked on the water. Only when he took his eyes off Jesus and began to notice the frightening circumstances around him did Peter fear and begin to sink. Even so, the Lord immediately caught him and helped him into the boat.

Yes, as you focus on Christ, you will have the faith you need to minister. And you will also have the amazing power of the Holy Spirit to strengthen you in ministry. For when Jesus calls you into ministry, He empowers you for that distinct ministry. All the strength and capability that you will need in helping others, the Holy Spirit will give to you. "Out of His glorious riches He may strengthen you with power through His Spirit" (Eph. 3:16). That same power that enabled Peter to get out of the boat and onto the water will enable you to get off the shore and into the water to help meet the needs of a hurting world.

If you had been there on the banks of the Potomac River that winter day in 1982 when the Air Florida jet crashed, would your eyes have been on the circumstances surrounding the crash – the frigid air, the icy waters – or on the Lord? Would the acknowledgment of Jesus Christ in your life have empowered you with the courage and faith to jump into that river, risking yourself to save others? Perhaps? If that sounds frightening, remember Peter's experience. When your eyes are on Christ, it can be done.

WE ARE CALLED TO CARE

We evangelical Christians need to remind ourselves that Jesus spoke to us of our need to be committed to two worlds- a lost world and a hurting world. In verses such as in Matthew 28:19-20 and Mark 16:15, we read the words of Jesus commanding us to minister to the lost who do not know His saving grace. And we obey.

Yet we choose to ignore other words of Jesus, such as those in Matthew 25:35-45, where He compares those who reach out to the hurting world with those who do not. And the comparison makes it very clear that He expects us to minister to those in this world as well. When Jesus said, "Whatever you did for one of the least of these brothers of mine, you did for me" (Matt. 25:40), He is reminding us of the many people who never hear an encouraging word, who never feel a kind hand, who never have a sense of companionship or relationship.

Ministering to the hurting *and* to the lost are both our responsibility.

Sadly, some Christians seem satisfied with not ministering to either world. They are content with just going to church. But Jesus not only called us into church, He also calls us out of church and into the world of need around us to minister in His name. As a distinguished Canadian churchman once reminded us, "God does not spend much time in church; He spends it in a hurting world."

So if our Christianity allows us to believe that Jesus is content for us to sit idly – and safely – on the shore, unconcerned about those around us who are drowning in need, we need to rethink what it means to be Christian. For called to be Christian means called to care. If not, why are we instructed by God's Word to "carry each other's burdens"? (Gal. 6:2)

WHEN SOMEONE CARES

Christians can learn something very important from two other groups in our society – cults and gangs. Does that sound surprising? Why are so many church groups in America today losing members while cults and gangs keep growing? Cults and gangs grow because hurting people with real needs believe those groups will care for them. And many of these same people believe the Church does not. And isn't it true that many of us evangelical Christians really don't care?

Maybe it is an old cliché that a drowning man will clutch at a straw. But that explains why people, unloved and uncared for, who are drowning in overwhelming circumstances clutch at the straw offered them by a cult or a gang. True, cults are theologically confused and gangs have a lawless life-style. But cults hold out the promise of acceptance, and gangs the promise of protection to their members. Even though in both groups, the loving and caring is basically a means to an end, their continued growth clearly proves a point that we Christians must understand – people need to know that someone loves and cares for them. And they will respond to and identify with those who demonstrate that kind of care – even when the "caring" is given for the wrong reasons.

I once heard a talk show host interviewing four gang members. The youngest of the four was only 11 years old. The host asked this child, "If your gang told you to steal, would you steal?"

"Yes, I would," the child replied.

The host next asked him, "If they asked you to beat somebody up, would you do this? Would you beat a person up – another young person?"

"Yes, I would."

Then the interviewer asked, "How about if they asked you to murder someone, would you really do that?"

Without hesitation, the young boy answered, "Yes, I would."

The host's chin dropped to his chest as his mouth opened wide in astonishment. He couldn't believe the answer he had just heard. So he asked one further question, "How could you actually do something like that?"

Looking directly at his interviewer, the 11-year-old said, "When you're cared for, you'll do just about anything. My own family – they don't care if I come or go; they don't care what I do. My dad isn't even around anymore. The only people who really care for me are the group of guys I'm with. And whatever they ask me to do – I'll do it, 'cause *when you're cared for you'll do almost anything."*

Again, the chief reason why these street gangs and religious cults are growing is that their members believe they are genuinely cared for. And when people are cared for, they'll join almost anything – and do almost anything. Gangs and cults have realized the tremendous power that encouragement and support hold.

Both groups have members who know what it means to risk themselves for one another. That is why they are able to command an outstanding allegiance from their members. This shows what happens to people when someone gives a hand of support to them. If you got off the shore and gave your hand of support to someone, think of the impact you could have!

Fortunately for a lady who was a passenger on a 1988 Aloha Airlines flight, the gentleman sitting next to her reached out to her and risked himself to save her life. The plane had been in the air only a short time when suddenly a huge part of its upper fuselage tore away while the plane was flying over the ocean near Hawaii. As that section of the plane ripped away, a stewardess was sucked overboard and killed.

Somehow, the plane continued flying and the pilots were able to land it safely back at the Honolulu airport where the flight had begun. There a male passenger told that he was sitting in his seat with his laptop computer as the plane split open above him. His computer and everything else not fastened down was sucked right out of the plane.

In the window seat beside him sat a lady. As the fuselage came apart next to her, she looked out and saw nothing between her and the blue ocean below. Nothing at all. The man said, "This lady grabbed hold of me so tightly – and she wasn't about to let go." And, he added, "I grabbed her too, and I held onto her knowing that if she goes out the side of the plane, so do I."

Now that's beautiful. He didn't know who she was except that she was another human being in terrible need. And, despite the risk to himself, he got off the shore and into the water. And, in doing so, he undoubtedly rescued her. Now that's a true stretcher-bearer.

If you are already off the shore and into the water, swimming toward someone who's drowning. God bless you. That means you are already responding to someone's desperate need. Is the water often cold? Yes. Are there currents? You bet. And it takes a great deal of effort and strength to continue? It does, but you do so because you know it's worth the risk.

You have already seen that real life is out in the water and that out there we all really need each other. But, I will hold on to you. And you, please, hold on to me. For together we will safely make the shore.

PERSONAL TIME

A. Many times there is no answer to the cry for help.
Describe: _____

_____

In your opinion, why is it difficult for some people to offer encouragement and assistance at such times?_____

_____

B. Can you think of practical ways to care for and encourage someone you know who is on a stretcher? _____

_____

_____

Remember, when a person is cared for, he or she will do just about anything for those providing the caring.

GRAB A HANDLE

As you look into the mirror today, realize that you can make a change in your world. You can lift stretchers of hurting people. Change takes place as you help to make it happen.

Do you remember the drawing of the stretcher in chapter 2? You were to write your name in the middle of the stretcher and then think of four people who would lift or carry this stretcher and write their names down – one at each of the stretcher's four corners. Take a minute now to recall the people that came into your mind. Were there just one or two, or were you able to think of three or four?

What if you were unable to think of any particular person who would carry your stretcher? If this is true, do not be upset or worried, for I believe two things might be occurring.

1. *God may be demonstrating to you that you need first to reach out to others.* We all need people in our lives, yet sometimes it is very difficult to admit to other persons that we need their assistance or help. Maybe what you need to do is to risk yourself honestly by reaching out to a special person or close family member and tell that one you need his or her help. It can be difficult at first, but it has the potential of turning your difficulty into a heartwarming experience, not only for you, but for the person who is able to assist you during this stretcher time. God uses this tremendous biblical principle regarding the ministry and support of others through each one of us.

2. *There will be some stretcher times in life that we will be called upon to face alone.* The assistance of that special friend of Proverbs 18:24 – that stretcher-bearer – just won't be there for one reason or another. Indeed, there might well be those hard stretcher times in life where we would dearly love to have that close friend, that mother or father, that husband or wife, that pastor or counselor

there to be part of this hard situation, yet we are called upon to face it alone. The reason is not that we don't have friends who will uphold us and lift our stretchers, it just happens that there are times when we have to "go it alone." I have named those times when no one is around to assist us as "Gethsemane moments."

THE MEANING OF GETHSEMANE

Are you recalling or thinking of the Gethsemane that Jesus experienced? Before we look into that story to learn some valuable insights about Gethsemane, I want to give you a practical definition that would benefit you to remember. *Gethsemane moments are those difficult times and places in life, we have to face and many times alone.*

Gethsemane times are hard places where life seems to have given us much more than we can bear or handle. They are the hard times we wish would go away so we could finally fall asleep at night.

We want to wake up in the morning and find the difficulty is gone. Except that is not usually what happens. We wake up in the morning to find the same difficult situation, that hard place, that stretcher-bearing time is still there.

In facing our own personal Gethsemanes, we often would rather have our difficulties just disappear or go away. There are many problems that we simply do not want to face. Sometimes we find ourselves wishing so badly that they had never happened, but we start another day, another week and they are still before us.

I know personally that there have been times in my own life where I wished for certain situations to disappear. I had asked the Lord to take them away, but when I awoke the next day, they were still there. Those hard times had to be faced whether I wanted to face them or not.

Even now you might be feeling the same way. You might be in a situation today where you can say, "He is so right, I do wish for this situation in my life to go away, except it hasn't."

It can be frightening, when you suddenly find there is a hard situation that you must face – all alone. I don't know about you, but I know I would much rather have people around me that could assist, advise and help me. To be alone in a Gethsemane situation or in a stretcher time can make the problem even more difficult and, like it or not, we have no real choice but to try our best to face the problem.

Many people find they can relate to this definition of Gethsemane in a very realistic way. Can you? Think of past moments in your own life that you could now label as "Gethsemane moments." Think also of any situation in your life that is occurring right now that you would label as a Gethsemane time.

MY GETHSEMANE

One of those hard times and places for me was Viet Nam. Yes, there were friends, my parents and other close family members behind me in love, support and prayer. Yet, it was I alone who had to board that jet for Viet Nam; no one could come with me.

My Time In Viet Nam

I naturally met other men there, but most were as scared and lonely as I was. Many had turned to drinking and drugs to help combat those feelings. The drinking and drug problems among the young men over there were enormous. The problem continued to grow, not necessarily because these young men enjoyed the drinking or the drugs, but because they felt the need to find a way to escape. They wanted to be able to forget the Gethsemane they were in – this Viet Nam and the war.

A man would drink two six-packs at night when he was not on patrol, or smoke as much marijuana as he wanted and – for a moment maybe – he could forget where he was. But in the morning he woke up, still in the same place with the same sound of bullets and bombs and death all around him.

This hard time in their lives had to be faced alone. They wished it would go away, and for a small amount of time, it seemed to them that the drugs and the alcohol were the answer to their Gethsemanes. Viet Nam hurt just as much for me, and I too wished it would go away. Yet, it did not.

My Trip To Viet Nam

I remember certain things about this specific time, like getting the orders that sent me to Viet Nam. I remember boarding a jet out of Seattle knowing that 19 hours later I would land in Viet Nam. On the way over, I sat silently in my seat, spending little time talking to anyone. I kept thinking and trying to visualize the land and the area I would find myself fighting in and around during the next year. I couldn't help wondering at times different things such as, would I die? Would I be injured? Would I ever see my parents, my brother, my friends again?

As I thought deeper about my situation, I found I was becoming more and more scared, lonely and upset toward God. Prior to all this, positive things had been happening in my life regarding my relationship with Jesus Christ. At 19 years of age, I had given my life to Him as never before. My desire to grow and my commitment to live out a life-style in Jesus Christ were very real.

Yet, I couldn't help but think about the situation I was in, and I found I was really angry. It seemed to me that since I had given my life to Jesus in sincerity, I should not have been on this jet on the way to Viet Nam! I felt it really wasn't fair, and I was definitely angry.

However, when we were leaving the Philippines on the last part of our flight, I sensed then that the Lord already was responding to my needs, and I felt Him helping me deal with anger, the loneliness and frustration I was feeling. In my heart,

I heard Him say, "Michael cannot the God that I am, the powerful God, the caring God that you have fallen in love with in Glendale, be the same powerful and caring God in Viet Nam? Is my love and power and my caring confined within the boundaries of California?

These were very difficult questions to answer. Yet they had to be answered honestly and within the next few hours. You see, Gethsemane was approaching. This gave me time to wrestle with these questions. Finally the answers came. He would be the God of the present, and if the present was Viet Nam instead of California, He would be there.

AN UNDERSTANDING OF GETHSEMANE

Journey back with me to the Gethsemane our Lord Jesus Christ experienced. I want us to return to His Gethsemane, because as we do, we can learn some valuable insights into handling our own Gethsemanes – those hard, lonely times that can become part of our lives. In Matthew 26:36-46, we read:

> Then Jesus went with his disciples to a place called Gethsemane, and he said to them, "Sit here while I go over there and pray." He took Peter and the two sons of Zebedee along with him, and he began to be sorrowful and troubled. Then he said to them, "My soul is overwhelmed with sorrow to the point of death. Stay here and keep watch with me."

> Going a little farther, he fell with his face to the ground and prayed, "My Father, if it is possible, may this cup be taken from me. Yet not as I will, but as you will."

> Then he returned to his disciples and found them sleeping. "Could you men not keep watch with me

for one hour?" he asked Peter. "Watch and pray so that you will not fall into temptation. The spirit is willing, but the body is weak."

He went away a second time and prayed, "My Father, if it is not possible for this cup to be taken away unless I drink it, may your will be done."

When he came back, he again found them sleeping because their eyes were heavy. So he left them and went away once more and prayed the third time, saying the same thing.

Then he returned to the disciples and said to them, "Are you still sleeping and resting? Look, the hour is near, and the Son of Man is betrayed into the hands of sinners. Rise, let us go! Here comes my betrayer!"

The day that Jesus was to enter Gethsemane had to have been one of the most difficult, hard and lonely days in His life. He knew that the time with His friends was limited. He knew that in a few hours His freedom would be taken from Him and He would be arrested. And He knew He had been betrayed by a dear friend. He had just finished saying a special prayer (see John 17), a prayer concerning Himself, His disciples and His believers down through the ages.

He knew His work would soon be finished. It was the end of His preaching. He had disciplined Himself and had been completely obedient to His Father in sharing the Kingdom of God for three years. His miracles would now cease. His instructions had come to a conclusion. He now had said it all. In fact, He had said it all several times. He had barely 90 minutes of freedom left.

The Last Supper had been eaten, and Jesus and His disciples had gone up into the Mount of Olives. It had been one of their favorite places where the group could go, and now they all went there to rest, as they were very tired.

Jesus knew that now it was time for waiting. Alone perhaps, He walked through a nearby olive grove and thought back over His earthly life. As He reminisced, He probably thought about the time that He first met His disciples, the dear friends that would now be entrusted to carry on the work of the Master. He undoubtedly could have invited these friends to sit with Him and share the old stories, but instead, something prompted Him to go on inside the garden. He motioned to Peter, James and John, who were so special to Him. Could they be the stretcher-bearers in His life? He told them to follow Him, and they did. They walked outside the cave and across the road to the shadow of the olive garden. There the three stopped and Jesus now made ready to enter Gethsemane alone.

The Garden of Gethsemane was east of Jerusalem near the Mount of Olives and was filled with olive trees. It had become a favorite retreat for Jesus and His disciples. In the Gospels of Mark and Matthew, it is referred to as a "field." Luke simply calls it "the place." John identifies it as the "garden" and the Garden of Gethsemane." Our definition of Gethsemane? *What I experience when a hard time or place comes in my life and I must face it alone.*

As we have traced the journey of Jesus, Peter, James and John, we come now to the entrance of the garden. Jesus had motioned to Peter, James and John to sit and to remain, as He must now enter deeper into the garden alone. However, He still needed their assistance and their support. They were called to be His stretcher-bearers at a very critical and difficult time in our Lord's life. The coming experience was one that Jesus did not wish to face alone. He desired the support and encouragement of His friends.

Jesus became so overwhelmed with sadness and grief that He entreated His disciples to stay awake with Him, so He would be able to share with them how brokenhearted and grieved He was. He needed His friends at that moment.

And what happened? Jesus walked into the garden and began to talk earnestly with His Father. Then knowing fully how heavy the cup would be, He fell to the ground, asking that it be removed. And then the answer: no. Jesus finally said, "Not my will, but your will be done."

When Jesus returned to His stretcher-bearing friends, He found Peter, James and John all asleep. The previous day had been long. And it was now early the next morning; they had probably been up nearly 20 hours. They were tired He knew, but He had needed them. He woke them up and told them that the spirit was willing, but the flesh at times is very weak.

Jesus knew He needed a stretcher-bearer. He knew He needed His friends for support. But they had already failed Him by falling asleep. And they would fail Him again. He could not count on those He needed for support, and now He would have to face His Gethsemane all alone.

TWO THOUGHTS

Can this be like us? Many times when we are facing a very difficult situation, we share ourselves with a close friend who says he or she will be there, and then for some reason or circumstance, that one is simply not there. Or maybe we are just unable to find a friend to share with. Then, like Jesus, we are called to face our own Gethsemane all alone.

As a person goes through a Gethsemane experience, something often begins happening to that person inwardly. A sense of being very real and honest starts to generate within that person. Their innermost feelings and thoughts somehow become very pronounced. Everything they are sensing becomes much more open and alive. In other words, as a person goes through a Gethsemane experience, he or she finds it very hard to hide behind a mask. The real person comes to the forefront.

What can we learn from Him for this hard time in our life? How are we not only to face our Gethsemane, but also walk through it and finally leave it victoriously just as Jesus did? Continue to journey with me so that by learning from our Lord, we too can be victorious in the Gethsemanes of our lives.

KEYS TO HANDLING THE HARD & LONELY TIMES

If we study Jesus at this particular point in the Garden of Gethsemane, we are able to observe that not only did He have to cope with this very difficult situation, but He faced it with strength and courage. As we study these Scriptures further we are able to admire Him even more as He leaves the Garden of Gethsemane. Not only was He able to cope with and face this very hard place, but He was able to walk from the garden victoriously.

What enabled Jesus to walk from that garden victoriously? Can those same characteristics become part of our own lives? Can they be applied in such a way that we too are able not only to face our Gethsemanes, but walk through them victoriously? Can we leave our garden and be stronger than we ever were before, just as our Lord Jesus Christ did?

Take a long and searching look at Jesus in His garden. Notice the three characteristics that enabled Him to deal with His Gethsemane time.

The First Characteristic: Obedience

Obedience is defined as "yielding willingly to command; submissive to authority." That definition has implications we may not like very well. We find obedience both hard and difficult to put into practice in our daily lives.

"Going a little farther, he fell with his face to the ground and prayed, 'My Father, if it is possible, may this cup be taken from me. Yet not as I will, but as you will'" (Matt. 26:39).

Obedience was the very center of Jesus' life. It was the law of His life, He had a passionate love for His Father, and therefore He was consistently obedient in all He had been sent to do. His will was to do the will of Him who sent Him, not His own (see John 4:34). His obedience was costly, but abundantly fruitful.

Obedience to His Father's cause – that was always the theme of the life of Jesus, the essence of the drama He lived out totally. He was obedient in order to guide all who came after Him in the ways of truth and to show us there was light in the darkness. He wanted us to see how His obedience would enable us to believe when we would want to doubt. His obedience would be an encouragement to each one of us, an encouragement so we can move on.

What hinders our obedience? We need to examine ourselves. Why do we at times disobey? Why do we fail to fulfill the obedience we are called to? Matthew 26:41 gives us the answer. Jesus had just said to Peter, "Watch and pray, so that you don't fall into temptation. The spirit is willing, but the body, the flesh is so weak" (author paraphrase).

In Romans 7:14-25 (*KJV*), the Apostle Paul describes "the flesh." "The flesh:" is used to define our human condition. It is that frail, mortal, natural self. Each one of us has that flesh.

Paul's description of "the flesh" is interesting, and his struggles with "the flesh" can be of help to us as Christians. We are subjected daily to alternative situations which are counter to and challenge our Christian life-style. This conflict can create stress points in our daily living, as we have to make choices.

On one side is our redeemed self in Jesus Christ. The redeemed self has the services of the Holy Spirit for each one of us. On the other side is the fact that we have to live out this redeemed self in the middle of a sinful world full of temptations, emotional turmoils, mixed feelings, bad influences – and Gethsemanes.

This journey of life we travel can be extremely difficult at times. But as Christians in the process of sanctification, we must somehow live out that journey to the fullest. The hard part is that we must live it out in the middle of this sinful world. We cannot live out our Christianity in a beautiful greenhouse setting, knowing the air is filtered and clean, where there are perfect solar conditions and no weeds are allowed to grow.

Paul knew what it meant to be subjected to this world's temptations and bad influences. He understood the words of Jesus, knew what it meant to have the flesh fight the spirit. He had the desire to do the godly things, the right things, and to follow through on the obedience he had been called to. But he found he also needed to question himself. "Why, why, do I not do those things I should? Why at times do I fail and begin to do the things I do not want to do?" Paul knew the stress of being obedient. He felt the "pressure points:" we feel as we try to live out that Christian life-style in the middle of a sinful world.

As Christians we need to develop within ourselves the desire to be obedient. We need to make it become our will, within the center of our hearts as Jesus did. It is a difficult task and we need to strive toward this achievement with all the strength we have. We need to take our feelings, our emotions and our Gethsemanes and live them out in that city, that town, that state, that world we are so much a part of. We must not quit. We must be obedient to the truth in the Word of God. We must conduct ourselves in such a manner that we can be at peace with our choices.

As the desire to be more Christlike and to be more obedient grows, we need to be aware that at times it will be quite difficult to follow through, as obedience will not necessarily make life any easier. Now, that might sound like a contradiction to you. As you seek God, why doesn't life become easier? Won't being Christlike and seeking His will with all our hearts create an easier world for us to be a part of?

Not necessarily.

You see, your desire to become that man or woman of God alerts Satan that you, as a person in Christ, have the potential and the power to influence others for Jesus. Such a possibility upsets Satan so much that he will want to discourage, defeat and destroy you.

If we, Sunday after Sunday, are just sitting in our pew, not excited about a life-style in Jesus Christ, not desiring that obedience, not worrying if we fail; if we have the attitude that says, "Well, we all sin don't we? We all fail, none of us are perfect!" Then we play straight into the hand of Satan, He now knows we are not a threat to him. But if instead, we say we want to be that man of God, that woman of God and be obedient to the truth, the truth of God, Satan knows he must now begin to influence our lives. When he does go into action be very aware, because he will try everything he can to destroy you and to discourage you. That is why it's at the times when we are sincerely seeking obedience and to be more Christlike, that life often becomes more difficult.

The Second Characteristic: The Will

The second key we have been given in handling these hard Gethsemane times can be found in Matthew 26:42: "He went away a second time and prayed, 'My Father, if it is not possible for this cup to be taken away unless I drink it, may your will be done.'"

We find here that the second ingredient we need to handle the hard places in our lives is the will. We can define the word "will" as: the power by which the mind decides upon and directs its energies to carry out an action.

The will is that mental attitude that says, "I am going to do it, I'm going to do this no matter what the cup is. I'm going to follow through and drink of it." As you are reading this book, you may be feeling that you are drinking from some of the hardest cups of your life; hard cups of life that you wish could be taken away from you. These could be the cup of divorce, the cup of death, the cup of longing for companionship, the cup of guilt. All these separate and distinct cups of hardships can go on and on. For some of you, you have no choice at all but to drink of them. Then you must move on with a strength that says, I will see this all the way through.

My will vs. your will. A very important point we must clearly understand is, someone else's will cannot be your will. You can gather from a friend complete support and encouragement, but when it comes down to the point of desire, determination and decision – the will, it must be from within yourself. It must be your very own.

I cannot will something for you. You must will it for yourself. A mother, father, brother, sister, or pastor cannot will something for you. You must will it for yourself.

Peter, James and John could not enter into the inner Garden of Gethsemane with Jesus. Even though they were there, even if they had stayed awake, their will could not become Jesus' will. Jesus had to will it for Himself, not only to drink of that cup, but to follow through. Someone else's will cannot be yours. You must desire it yourself.

Earlier, I told you about a young woman named Lisa. I explained how she had been extremely sick when she was pregnant and how she had lost a great deal of weight. I remember those visits with her in the hospital and how hard it was for her not to be discouraged, as she said the same prayers over and over again. I could not seem to instill within her that desire which would enable her to grab onto her own inner personal will and be able to say, "I'm going to make it through this. Before I know it my child will be born."

What is also interesting, as much as I desired for her sickness to pass and the child to be born to her and her husband, Keith, my own desire, my own will was not able to take root

within Lisa. Only she herself would be able to finally come to
that point and will it for herself with all her heart. To be able to
pass through this hard time, this Gethsemane, she had to accept
and say, "I will drink of this cup and see the birth of this child
– no matter what." To see Lisa able to come to that point was
exciting. She did develop for herself the will and the desire to
drink of the cup.

One of life's hardest tasks is to accept what we cannot understand, or to accept what seems to make little sense to us.
We wonder why we have to go through Gethsemanes and to
have cups that taste so bitter. We need to understand that we
are human in nature; therefore, we have those human emotions and feelings. When we find that at times we do not get
things our way, or the Lord just does not do what we ourselves have in mind, our human emotions then begin to take
over. And what do they do? They can cause us to compromise;
they can cause us to be disobedient; and they can cause us to
want to quit.

What makes us want to compromise is when our will and
our obedience are taken over by our flesh. Remember, these
are the desires, the appetites of the self, the emotions, and
they now begin to rule us. The truth that God is there and
can set us free becomes shadowed somehow and secondary to
our nature.

However, we must be vitally aware that we cannot compromise. During those hard and lonely times, we must somehow
remain obedient as our Lord did. We need only to develop that
desire, that will within ourselves that allows us to follow through,
remembering inwardly to say, "I will trust in God's faithfulness,
especially during this Gethsemane of my life. I know as I drink
of this cup, God is supplying me with adequate strength and
courage so that there will be a new tomorrow and the cup will
finally pass."

The Third Characteristic: The Follow Through

Matthew 26:46 contains the key to not only handling our Gethsemanes, but walking through them. "Rise, let us go! Here comes my betrayer!"

The last step in handling any Gethsemane experience is "the follow through." Follow through is probably the hardest point to handle when you must deal with a Gethsemane. The follow through says, "I now take on the responsibility of my obedience, and my desire, no matter what, is to arise and drink of that cup."

Jesus, at the moment in His life, as He dealt with His Father alone in the garden, could have remained there defeated. He could have disappeared. Or, He could have allowed Himself just to die a good prophet of love, to be known only as a good man who had done good things, a man whose stories might have been retold years later. But, He chose not to die as just a good prophet. He chose not to die a storyteller. He chose to die as the Son of God. He knew He would die as the Son of God at the moment He left Gethsemane, and He chose to follow through.

As you recall His story, when He left the Garden of Gethsemane, His life did not become any easier. He was arrested, His close friends deserted Him, one had even betrayed Him. He was falsely accused, He went through the mockery of a trial, He was spit upon, He was crowned with thorns, He was made fun of, He was beaten upon the head, He was whipped 39 times. He even had to bear the knowledge that Peter, one of His closest friends, would deny that he had ever known Him.

Jesus then went to be crucified, the weight of the cross so heavy, it caused Him to fall when He still had a third of the way to go up to Calvary. But, He picked Himself up, looked up at the hill called Golgotha then continued to walk all the way to the top.

Three tremendous blows followed as nails were driven into each hand and through the feet. Later, He looked down from that cross upon His mother. He knew in a few moments He must leave her and leave all the friends He loved so dearly.

We need to understand that, even as Christ followed through this Gethsemane, the events did not get any easier; they got harder and harder. But, He did continue on, not only in obedience, but with an inner will that only He Himself could control. He still continued to follow through, right on through to His own death.

Then three days later, there was the New Beginning, as He came back victorious. He had conquered death, Satan and all the principalities. He had left Gethsemane behind and followed through.

THE POWER IS IN THE FOLLOW THROUGH

I want to share a statement that is so meaningful and inspirational in regards to the follow through. The statement is, "the power is in the follow through." I want to repeat it again, "the power is in the follow through." The power being the outcome or the results of the situation.

To truly understand this statement let us consider athletes and their sport of participation. If they are to succeed or achieve, no matter what the sport, they are taught the power and the need to follow through.

If you are a golfer, keep your head down and follow through on your swing. If you are a basketball player, extend your arm and follow through. If you are a baseball player, follow through and swing if you are to hit the ball. If you are a football player as a receiver, run your pattern. As a quarter back, you must follow through with your arm to complete the pass. If as a team you are to succeed everyone must follow through on their assignment. A breakdown on assignment can affect the whole team. Coaches get angry at players who do not follow through on their assignment.

I remember watching an interview with the former great baseball player Reggie Jackson. Reggie was one of the all time great players that played professional baseball. He even went by the nickname, "Mr. October." This title was given to him for his performance during the playoffs and world series that took place every October. He was known for his clutch hitting and power of his home runs.

During an interview that took place after he had retired, Reggie was taking questions about his career in baseball from various reporters. One young reporter stood up and asked Reggie the following question. "How does it feel to know you struck out more times in your career than most of the people that played baseball?" After the question was stated out loud a quiet hush came over the room. Some of the older reporters looked at the young reporter in disbelief. How could he ask Reggie such a personal, hard question. Reggie was also known at times for his temper. Many in the room thought, Reggie is going to break this young reporter like a pencil.

Reggie looked at the young reporter and asked him to repeat the question. Once again he stated it, "How does it feel to know you struck out more times in your career than most of the people that played baseball?" For a moment they just looked at each other. Reggie finally spoke. "It does not bother me at all." The young reporter snapped back, "it really does not bother you at all?" Reggie looked back at him and said no. But let me tell you what bothered me a lot when I played baseball. Reggie stood up and said the following:

"What bothered me the most was when I went to bat and in the process a third strike was called out on me and I never took a swing. The ball came over the plate. The umpire called strike three you're out and the bat was still sitting on my shoulder. I did not even swing at the ball. The pitcher did not get me out. I got myself out.

"Now I have to walk back to the dugout where my team-mates are and my bat in resting on my shoulder. That bothered me so much. Young man," Reggie said, "the issue in life and baseball is not strike three but the position of your bat. I can return to the dugout knowing I swung. The pitcher just got me out this time. I will be back and get a hit next time." We all strike out. That is not the important factor. What is so important is the swing and the follow through. For that is where you have success and get the hits.

JESUS OUR EXAMPLE

With Jesus as our example, we need to realize that what was true for Him is true for us in our Christian faith and walk, especially during our Gethsemane times. There is no shortening of this race, but we must run it and endure the stress of running all the way to the finish. We start at point *A* and we continue until we get to point *B*. The hardest will be what is between those two points.

Imagine a marathon race. The start isn't too hard and once you see the finish line, that isn't too hard either. What is difficult is what takes place in between – all those miles where you run alone with sweat pouring off your brow and a fierce ache in your side! That's where the race is run – in between. Call it the follow through.

A WORD OF ENCOURAGEMENT

I don't know if you are going through a Garden of Gethsemane experience. I don't know if one of your friends is experiencing a hard and lonely time. You and I know, no matter who we are, such times must be faced.

We are probably alike in wanting someone to point us to the exit sign and say, "Here, this is the way out." More than likely, we would both run through that door. But my friend, at times there is no exit sign, and those hard times just won't go away.

Yet I assure you, you can make it. You really can make it. And you, friends, can make it too. With stretcher-bearers, you can make it.

There will also be those times when there just isn't a stretcher-bearer to help you. But even then you can still get through this hard time alone. Just remember to commit yourself to the principles our Lord used in His own garden experience, and you too can make it through your Gethsemanes. You need never remain there defeated.

Put to work the principles our Lord taught us in His garden experience:

Be obedient. Be obedient to the truth from the Word of God and believe in the faithfulness of His promises.

Will to know and do His will. Pray that God will develop within you the desire to have the will you need, the will to say, "May your will be done." Remember, no one else can give this desire to you. You must desire it for yourself. Then...

Follow through. Follow through without quitting. Run the race from point *A* to point *B* and, as it gets difficult, remember, there is a finish line. Also, the power is in the follow through.

Whether the cup passes or you are asked to drink it, determine to follow through in His strength. When you walk through the garden in His strength and in His will, the outcome is always victorious. Yes, each one of us can be successful in Gethsemane experiences – those hard places in our lives when we must "face it" all alone.

A WORD OF COMFORT

And now a word of comfort for those times when people let us down. There are times when people fail us and just are not there for us when we need them, just as Peter, James and John – choosing sleep over support – were not there for our Lord in His hour of need.

At such times in your life, Luke 22:43 should help and comfort you. While Jesus' disciples slept and left Him alone, "An angel from heaven appeared to him and strengthened him." How good to know that even though your stretcher bearers simply are not there for you, you are never entirely alone. God Himself is always there and will comfort you.

You can be alone physically, but never alone spiritually. Remember, you are not only a physical being, you are a spiritual being also. When you are in Christ, the Spirit of God lives within you (see I Cor. 3:16) and is your Comforter (see John 14:26.)

Jesus promised you, "I will be with you always, to the very end of the age" (Matt. 28:20). And "God has said, 'Never will I leave you; never will I forsake you" (Heb. 13:5). So you can take comfort from the knowledge that God will never abandon you in your Gethsemane moment. Even if, in your garden, you must drink of the cup. Jesus will drink the cup with you. And together you will walk through and leave the garden victoriously.

For me, this word of comfort became evident in Viet Nam. I had left my family and friends behind. They could not travel and be with me in those jungles. Yet God did not remain within the comfortable boundaries of California. The same living, powerful, caring God I knew in California had journeyed with me to Viet Nam. He would minister to me and never leave or forsake me. Gethsemane had now become a strengthening, growing time in my life.

PERSONAL TIME

A. Think of a time in your life that you would consider a Gethsemane moment. Explain_____

_____

_____

B. How do you grow or what did you learn from your Gethsemane moment? _____

_____

C. Which key do you find the hardest to turn in your life?

Key   *Why*

_____   _____

_____   _____

How can you strengthen that key? _____

_____

_____

Have you noticed how crowded the stores are becoming? Everywhere, people are bumping into each other as they rush about. And, it seems as though the stores are out of whatever it is you might want. Or, someone else has just beaten you to it. Another thing I've noticed - they just don't make stores large enough anymore. Have you noticed this as well? The aisles are so small and crowded it seems to be hard to get your cart up and down.

I would like to ask what you might think about our roads and freeways? Have you been aware of how congested they are and of how much longer it seems to take to get home? The roads are so crowded that I couldn't reach the maximum speed limit if I tried. I don't think we've ever had so many different types of cars and from so many foreign countries. How in the world are we going to have enough gas for all these cars in the upcoming years?

Families are really growing too. Have you noticed that? Especially around the holiday times, there seems to be more gifts to buy? You keep hearing that another child was born. And someone always has a new grandson or a granddaughter. Maybe your own family has been increasing too.

The fact is, and what I am really trying to say is, that there are people all around us, aren't there? It's the "population explosion" or whatever you may want to call it. Yet, even with all these people, it is very evident how impersonal life can be. Yes, we're always running into one another and we rub shoulders as we pass. With those we meet, we shake hands and sort of say, "Hi," but are we really aware of one another?

Have you ever found yourself wondering if anyone really knows that you exist? Or, more importantly, does your existence really matter to them? Have you personally known anyone who might have said, "I go to church and there are people all around me. The gospel is being preached, songs are being sung, but does anyone hear what I say or the song I sing? If I didn't attend church for the next month, would anyone care? Would someone give me a call? Would I be missed?"

Pressures such as these begin to build up inside people today. Both in the world and, unfortunately, within the Christian community, many people just do not feel supported and encouraged. Sadly, they felt they are just numbers, just numbers in this game called life.

A SPIRITUAL CANCER

The inability to encourage and support others could be defined as a spiritual cancer. All by itself it has the ability to cause tremendous problems because it so often is undetected. It also can affect people from all walks of life, tragically even creeping into Christian organizations and working its way inward to the hearts of many dynamic churches. Yes, the inability to encourage and support others is a spiritual cancer and it can cause people to fail in their relationships.

This kind of pressure can build to a point where some people finally fall apart. Songwriter Neil Diamond has captured the feelings of many lonely, unloved people in this composition, "I am...I said." In this song, he tries to let someone, anyone, know who he is.

"I am," he says, but there is no one to hear, because there is no one to care. He is alone, so no one – no even a chair – hears him say, "I am." Toward the end of the song, he voices a cold and frightening thought: he has never cared for the sound of being alone. Then once again, with no one at all to hear, not even a chair, he affirms to a silent, empty room, "I am."

With this song, Neil Diamond has expressed the feeling – and sound – of loneliness. He tells of someone looking for a relationship with a friend. This friend could be a stretcher-bearer who would listen, who would care and who would support.

This someone walks around in his lonely world, unable to find that friend. By himself in his empty room – a defeated, lonely and discouraged man – he finds himself talking to a piece of furniture, a chair. Have you ever been in that room? Do you know anyone else who has been in that room, talking to something rather than to someone?

Is anyone really listening? Does anyone care for me? Many find they are asking such questions today. They are asking for support and encouragement. They need a stretcher-bearer. People just like you and me are in desperate need of having a personal relationship with someone.

In reaffirming the ministry of stretcher bearing here, I want now to share another concept that can have a very positive effect on your life and the lives of others. In John 11:1-44, you will find the story of a family on stretchers. As you read this account of their story, use your imagination to capture its underlying meaning and purpose.

> Now a man named Lazarus was sick. He was from Bethany, the village of Mary and her sister Martha. This Mary, whose brother Lazarus now lay sick, was the same one who poured perfume on the Lord and wiped his feet with her hair. So the sisters sent word to Jesus, "Lord, the one you love is sick."

> When he heard this, Jesus said, "This sickness will not end in death. No, it is for God's glory so that God's Son may be glorified through it." Jesus loved Martha and her sister and Lazarus. Yet, when he heard that Lazarus was sick, he stayed where he was two more days.

Then he said to his disciples, "Let us go back to Judea."

"But Rabbi," they said, "a short while ago the Jews tried to stone you, and yet you are going back there?"

Jesus answered, "Are there not twelve hours of daylight? A man who walks by day will not stumble, for he sees by this world's light. It is when he walks by night that he stumbles, for he has no light."

After he said this, he went on to tell them, "Our friend Lazarus has fallen asleep; but I am going there to wake him up."

His disciples replied, "Lord, if he sleeps, he will get better." Jesus had been speaking of his death, but his disciples thought he meant natural sleep.

So then he told them plainly, "Lazarus is dead, and for your sake I am glad I was not there, so that you may believe. But let us go to him."

Then Thomas (called Didymus) said to the rest of the disciples, "Let us also go, that we may die with him."

On his arrival, Jesus found that Lazarus had already been in the tomb for four days. Bethany was less than two miles from Jerusalem, and many Jews had come to Martha and Mary to comfort them in the loss of their brother. When Martha heard that Jesus was coming, she went out to meet him, but Mary stayed at home.

"Lord," Martha said to Jesus, "If you had been here, my brother would not have died. But I know that even now God will give you whatever you ask."

Jesus said to her, "Your brother will rise again."

Martha answered, "I know he will rise again in the resurrection at the last day."

Jesus said to her, "I am the resurrection and the life. He who believes in me will live, even though he dies; and whoever lives and believes in me will never die. Do you believe this?"

"Yes, Lord," she told him, "I believe that you are the Christ, the Son of God, who was to come into the world."

And after she had said this, she went back and called her sister Mary aside. "The Teacher is here," she said, "And is asking for you." When Mary heard this, she got up quickly and went to him. Now Jesus had not yet entered the village, but was still at the place where Martha had met him. When the Jews who had been with Mary in the house, comforting her, noticed how quickly she got up and went out, they followed her, supposing she was going to the tomb to mourn there.

When Jesus saw her weeping, and the Jews who had come along with her also weeping, he was deeply moved in spirit and troubled. "Where have you laid him?" he asked.

"Come and see, Lord," they replied.

Jesus wept.

Then the Jews said, "See how he loved him!"

But some of them said, "Could not he who opened the eyes of the blind man have kept this man from dying?"

Jesus, once more deeply moved, came to the tomb. It was a cave with a stone laid across the entrance. "Take away the stone," he said.

"But, Lord," said Martha, the sister of the dead man, "By this time there is a bad odor, for he has been there four days."

Then Jesus said, "Did I not tell you that if you be-lieved, you would see the glory of God?"

So they took away the stone. Then Jesus looked up and said, "Father, I thank you that you have heard me. I knew that you always hear me, but I said this for the benefit of the people standing here, that they may believe that you sent me."

When he had said this, Jesus called in a loud voice, "Lazarus, come out!" The dead man came out, his hands and feet wrapped with strips of linen, and a cloth around his face.

Jesus said to them, "Take off the grave clothes and let him go."

After reading this story, there are two special features we now need to focus our attention upon.

First, this family obviously sensed a real need for God to be personally involved in their lives. They needed to feel His personal touch, His personal concern, and they wanted to feel His love and care at this hard stretcher time.

Second, Jesus has vividly demonstrated within this story, how this family not only needed Him, but they also needed other people supporting them during this hard time. They had needed stretcher-bearing people who wanted to get involved in this family's problem.

RELIVING THE STORY

The story of Jesus, Lazarus, Mary and Martha did not have its beginning here. The four evidently had been quite good friends for a long time. Jesus had formed a special relationship with the three, and they were all very close to one another.

Lazarus, who was a brother to Martha and Mary, had suddenly become gravely ill. He grew quite sick while Jesus was preaching in some neighboring villages. Both Mary and Martha realized that Lazarus could soon die. They knew that Lazarus had need of his doctors, but they also knew that he needed healing through the divine touch of God even more.

The sisters heard that Jesus was in a nearby village, so they sent word to Him to come right away because Lazarus was so sick. They felt sure He would respond to their friendship and to their urgent, critical need.

Let's relive this time with Mary and Martha. Can you imagine the emotional turmoil they both are feeling? They know word has been sent to Jesus, and since He is not that far away, they feel He will arrive quite soon. We can almost picture them looking down their dusty road, fully expecting Jesus to appear within a short time. As they are looking down that road, they anxiously anticipate His arrival. They are concerned and worried about Lazarus, yet their hopes are high because Jesus is surely on the way to help them.

We need now to use our imagination more vividly. We'll say that it is around 10 in the morning. They feel sure that within the next hour, Jesus is going to be there. Yet, it gets to be later and later. It's eleven, twelve, then one o'clock. The afternoon sun has gotten very hot, yet Jesus still has not appeared in the distance. The rest of the day passes slowly and then it becomes dusk. One last time they look up the road and there is still no sign of Jesus.

Try now to relate to how they probably felt. They knew that Jesus could have made the journey back to Bethany in just a few hours, yet He did not come. How have you felt at times when you have asked God for certain crucial answers, because of a hard situation in your life, and there doesn't seem to be an answer? Your prayers just seem to bounce off the ceiling.

Mary and Martha had started this day with mixed feelings of anxiety, yet high hopes, with their feelings being uplifted by the good thoughts of Jesus coming to them. Then, by evening time, they are both disheartened. Their doubts now cause them to wonder. Is Jesus coming?

They probably slept restlessly that night and awoke the next morning to look once again down that road. Still no sign of Jesus. Hour after hour went by and once again, the day was more than half gone. The late afternoon sun caused lengthening shadows to appear. As it settled behind the horizon, and it became dusk, another day had ended. And still no Jesus.

Day after day went by. And Jesus did not come. How did they feel? It can be so very hard to wait upon the Lord and His timing.

From the Scriptures, we know that word of Lazarus being ill had reached Jesus. Giving His reasons (see John 11:4), Jesus chose to remain where He was. Then finally, He told His disciples that the ailing Lazarus had died (v. 14).

Through this death of Lazarus, Jesus intimated, something would happen which would make things clear to the disciples. In other words, He said, through the death of Lazarus, He was going to teach them to believe. He was trying to let them know that good would come from it. For now though, they were all to go to Bethany.

JESUS APPEARS

Jesus and His disciples made the journey and arrived at a place where Martha was waiting. She approached the Lord right away, saying, "Why didn't you come when we first sent for you?" (see v. 21). Martha was upset. She thought the Lord's timing was completely off base. If only He had been there! She knew if He'd been there, her brother would not have died. Yet, though she questioned Jesus' timing, Martha affirmed her faith in Him.

Martha then returned home and told Mary she had seen Jesus. Mary then rushed to where Jesus was. Her first words to the Lord were identical to Martha's opening remark: "Lord, if you had been here, my brother would not have died" (compare vv. 21 and 32).

Jesus became deeply moved and began to cry. Was He crying because of the pitiful situation, because of the people's unbelief or because of His own tenderness and human warmth?

Word circulated immediately that Jesus had arrived, and a large crowd gathered around Him. Some looked at Him and said, "Look how He cries. He cares so much, such a loving Lord." But a few in the crowd were skeptical, as if to say, "Some miracle worker! We hear He opened the eyes of a blind man, yet He couldn't come in time to save His friend from dying. Don't tell me you think He is the one who cares and loves. If He really cared for Lazarus, He would have come in time, and He didn't. Because of His delay, Lazarus died."

TWO IMPORTANT TRUTHS

A certain scene is now set before us. Jesus is in the middle of what could be a very delicate situation. Before we can go any further in this story, it is important for us to understand two dynamic truths:

Truth Number One: Jesus always deals with the main issue of a problem. Our responsibility is to *support* Jesus as He's dealing with the main issue. It is very important that we keep the thought of this first truth in mind while we look at Truth Number Two.

Truth Number Two: It is our responsibility to deal with the secondary issue of a problem. The inspiration for what we need to do in this regard comes to us through the power of the Holy Spirit. Our commitment to Jesus then helps us to follow through.

Main Issues

From our story, let's look at Truth Number One:

1. Death – resurrection (v. 14)
2. Eternal life – salvation (v. 21)

Remember you and I do not have the gift or power of raising someone from the dead. That is for God alone to resolve or decide upon.

Second, you and I do not have the power to give someone eternal life and to grant that person the forgiveness of sin. Why? Because I am a sinner and you are a sinner. We are all saved only by the grace of Jesus Christ (see Eph. 2:8-9). None of us can forgive sin. Only Christ can. Salvation is His to give. He forgives. His blood cleanses.

And what is our responsibility? Ours is to be in *support* of Jesus as He responds to and works with the main issues. You see, even though it is true that you and I do not have the right to forgive someone of sin, we do have the right, the privilege and the responsibility to share the good news of Jesus Christ's forgiveness of sins. We are meant to share our knowledge from the Bible of His atoning blood. His death on the cross and His resurrection, so that, through their acceptance of Jesus Christ, others also will have eternal life.

We need to realize that it is a privilege to witness, to invite our friends to church to hear the Gospel message; to give our personal testimony that we have been set free through Jesus Christ and have been born again. It is very important that we understand our own critical part here. Jesus *deals with the main issue* while we *support* the main issue.

I do not knowingly have the special gift of healing, yet I do know I can have the gift of faith. I can take the time to pray over someone and I can also anoint that person with oil, then believe Scripture with all my heart. It is still the job of Jesus, however, to heal. He must be the one to bring someone back to life who may have died on the operating table. We have all probably heard conversations or read articles about "out of body experiences." If they are true, it was still God alone who allowed that person to return to life.

As an example, in our church we had prayed for several weeks about a dear lady who was gravely ill. We prayed with all our hearts believing God would hear our prayers and restore her to health. As she lay in a coma I anointed her with oil, people in our church supported the family in various ways of ministry as well as in prayer. The seizures still continued to convulse her body, and it seemed inevitable that there would be brain damage.

We did support the family and we did support the main issue, as well as we could. The main issue was healing. The healing itself, however, was up to the Lord. It makes me extremely happy today to be able to say that the lady lived. God, from out of His grace and wonder, and to the amazement of her doctors and nurses, restored her to her family and her friends.

Secondary Issues

In the story about the raising of Lazarus, we consider Truth Number Two. His family knew they needed God to deal with the main issues. They also knew they needed people just like you and me to deal with the secondary issues. Jesus was so clear in His teaching. The responsibility of a stretcher-bearer is to deal with secondary issues. In this story there were three requests from Jesus, asking for the involvement of people. Can you recall what these three requests were?

The first is found in John 11:34. Jesus had asked the people, "Where have you laid him (Lazarus)?" Now, we know that God is all knowing. Therefore, have no doubt that He knew where Lazarus was. Right here, however, He has given us all a message. He was making it clear that it was their job (and our job) to become involved. And Paul said, "Bear ye one another's burdens, and so fulfill the law of Christ" (Gal. 6:2, *KJV*).

Jesus asked the people for their involvement. The people now had two choices: either to tell Him where Lazarus was, or to tell Him to forget it. Personally, I feel that if He had not received a helpful answer from the crowd, He might possibly have left the scene. I really do believe this. They did respond correctly to Him, however, and told Jesus to follow and they would show Him where Lazarus was laid.

Then He asked for their second involvement. In John 11:39, He asked the people to remove the stone covering the cave where they had buried Lazarus. Right away there was a protest from Martha. "He's been dead four days, there is a tremendous odor" (see v. 39).

In other words, "What's the use?" Once again, I feel that, if the people had not removed the rock, as He has asked, Jesus would simply have gone on His way. Perhaps He would even have said, "You don't believe. Without your belief and involvement, this miracle will not be taking place."

However, the people did respond and they did remove the rock. Jesus, of course, simply could have ordered that rock, "Be gone," and it would have been gone. But, He wanted the involvement of people actively working within the lives of this family.

The Lord first prayed and then shouted in a loud voice, "Lazarus, come out!"

Let's pause here for a moment. Think about how you would react if you were among the crowd that day and you knew that the Lord had just asked a dead man to come out of his tomb? I know I would probably have been more than a little suspicious about what was going to take place.

But Lazarus did come out! He walked out very slowly for his body was tightly wrapped, head to toe, in burial cloth. He was bound up rather like a mummy, probably barely able to slide his feet forward a few inches at a time. I picture him coming just outside the cave and stopping. And there he stood. Can you imagine the crowd's reaction? Much murmuring certainly from astonished onlookers. "Is he really alive?" "Is this an illusion or what?" "Can I believe what I am seeing?"

Jesus now made His third request for people to become involved. In verse 44, He said, "Take off the grave clothes and let him go." In effect, He said, "Remove the bandages." Now I don't know about you, but had I been there, I don't think I would have volunteered for that job. I think I would have watched someone else go up to that body and unwrap those bandages.

Yet Jesus was serious about His request. He wanted them to see that Lazarus was still bound up. He still needed to be freed from the secondary issue – the bandages. It was just as if Jesus had said, "You unwrap him. This is a secondary issue, and it's your job to deal with it."

THOUGHTS ON SECONDARY ISSUES

I am convinced that whenever anyone is going through a hard stretcher time, upon examination, we would always find there is a main issue and there are secondary issues. The main issue is God's territory and we are to be supportive of Him. But, the secondary issues are what God holds us responsible for.

I have thought for a long time about secondary issues and I would like to share the following conclusions.

First, I believe it is the secondary issues that dishearten people. It is the secondary issue that "breaks the camel's back." Many people do not become disheartened over main issues alone, even over serious concerns as critical illness or death.

I sincerely believe what disheartens most people is when they find themselves wondering if anyone cares. Does anyone care that someone dear to me is ill or dying? Does anyone care about going to the hospital with me or helping me solve my resulting financial problems? Would someone write me a letter of encouragement? It's those secondary issues that dishearten people.

Second, it's the secondary issues that can open doors for ministry to others. These open doors allow for our involvement within their lives. In reference to the story of Lazarus, we do not know how many people were actually involved, but we do know there were more than just two or even three people who told Jesus where Lazarus had been laid. At His second request, how many people cut the bandages?

After his bandages were cut, can't you just feel the excitement as Lazarus began to hug people, and they were able to realize at last that he was alive? How did those people who had taken an active part in all this feel? We can almost hear them now, as one says, "Well, I told Jesus where Lazarus had been laid." Another, "I was one who helped remove the rock." And still another, "I cut the bandages." Suddenly, we are finding people excited because of their involvement in his hard time.

Friends, Jesus is teaching us dynamic truths through this story. He knew all about main issues and secondary issues. He knew that once we involve ourselves in secondary issues we open ourselves for blessings, feelings of achievement and better relationships, as well as the special inner feelings you gain from helping out a friend.

NICOLE'S ILLNESS

Earlier, you learned about my daughter Nicole's close encounter with crib death or Sudden Infant Death Syndrome. The concept of main issues and secondary issues allows me to review some important facts about our story. We need to distinguish what the main issue was in regard to Nicole's illness. We would all probably agree it was the healing of our daughter. According to what medical research has learned, crib death syndrome is caused because a certain portion of the baby's brain is yet underdeveloped. This particular part of the brain signals the lungs to breathe. When it is not yet fully developed, the child simply does not react and breathe. Our prayers were to have her brain respond properly so she could breathe normally.

Financial Issue

Think with me now on what the secondary issues were. Were there some issues that could have disheartened my wife and me? In order to help you understand this total concept, I want to give you some personal and honest answers.

One of the main secondary issues we faced was a financial strain. Just before Nicole was born we had carefully budgeted into our expenses the conversion of the extra bedroom into a nursery for our new baby. We had also calculated the medical costs for Nicole's birth. Although we were insured for 80 percent of this cost, the remaining 20 percent had to be our responsibility. Even though we were thankful for the part the insurance was to pay, it was still going to be costly for us. When these various expenses occurred and were added together, they proved quite a bit for us.

Suddenly, there we were at Children's Hospital in the Intensive Care Unit. Intensive Care itself for one week was expensive enough, but it also required individual nurses to be on duty with Nicole. The bills began running up faster than we could list them. Once again, we knew our insurance would cover the 80 percent, but we also knew the 20 percent would cut into what savings we had.

Another large cost we had, in addition to all the medical bills, was our own daily living expenses while lodging in a motel near Children's Hospital. My wife was nursing our baby and had to be available to feed Nicole every three hours. It was impossible to commute an hour's drive from our home to the hospital. The additional money required for the motel and our meals out strained us not only financially, but also emotionally. It just seemed too much on top of our other worries. Our financial picture was definitely a secondary issue.

During the latter part of that week, my wife and I had again been discussing our financial dilemma while we were out to lunch. We returned to the nursery and found a note attached to our daughter's crib. It was a message to telephone my secretary at the church. When I called her, she gave me some wonderful news. Through the deacons of our church, a check was being sent to us. It was to meet those living expenses we were incurring. We felt so grateful.

The following Sunday, something else unbelievable occurred which continues to uphold us. I was not able to be in church to preach that Sunday because of Nicole, so my associate took my place. He went before the congregation and told them about the progress Nicole was making. He then brought before the church, what he believed was a secondary issue for us, the financial strain we were under. Strangely, I had never mentioned this problem to him. But it had been something he had sensed himself.

A special offering was taken that morning and the congregation donated nearly $950 to help us. And only about 225 people were attending our church at that time. We were astounded and so extremely thankful. Later, when we received the final bill from

Children's Hospital, the amount of money that had been collected covered nearly every penny of the portion that we owed.

The financial issue was no longer a burden. The only issue we had was to be close to one another for our baby daughter. We were not to worry about other things. If you were to ask today, if I feel close to the people in our church, I can tell you honestly that we are a family. A family that really cares for one another and a family that does attempt to deal with secondary issues when any one of us is on a stretcher.

Special Baby-sitter

We had another secondary issue in regard to Nicole's illness. When we were able to bring our daughter home, she still was not considered to be out of danger. As a result, she had to wear a special sensor that was wired to a machine. The machine monitored her breathing, and an alarm would go off if she did not take a breath within 15 seconds.

The pressure had begun for us once again. It was another type this time – the emotional strain from always having to be on the alert to listen for that alarm was very hard. I could go to work each day, and that gave me diversion from this strain, but my wife had to stay home. She did not have the freedom to leave the baby even to take a shower. She had to be able to hear that alarm. It put tremendous pressure upon her.

Nicole was not to be considered out of danger until she was about six months old. Therefore, we were looking at a long time to live with that kind of tension.

A very special lady in our church somehow realized this was a secondary issue. She also knew that under these special circumstances, it would be very hard for us to find a baby-sitter to relieve my wife for short intervals. This dear lady approached me and said, "To allow you and your wife to be able to go out to dinner or to be alone for a few hours, I am going to learn this special baby CPR, so that I can stay and watch your daughter."

You can well imagine what this did for us. Once again, God used someone to figure out and resolve our secondary issue. From this experience we can all learn how other people feel when they are relieved of their secondary issues, because of what other self-motivated people can offer to do.

We now have a second child named Ashley. She also has symptoms of crib death, but not as severely as Nicole had. However, once again my wife is quite restricted because of the baby having to be on a monitor. As a result, six young married ladies of our church volunteered to take turns baby-sitting Ashley. Now my wife can attend church on Sundays. I taught them myself all the special baby CPR, and now, each Sunday, one of these ladies is watching our small daughter in the church office. They know what to do in case she would forget to breathe. If this volunteer effort had not been offered, it would be six to nine months before my wife could come to church on a Sunday.

Once again I stress, it is those secondary issues, which wear people down. It is always Jesus who must deal with the main issues, but it's you and I who are called to the vital ministry of secondary issues. You and I are the ones who have the opportunity to roll away stones, to cut and remove the bandages and lift the burdens of so many people. It's a wonderful experience to be involved with secondary issues and there are blessings waiting for all who participate.

The Man on the Stretcher

Remember the story (Mark 2) about the paralytic who had not walked for many years? In that story, what was the main issue? In that case as well, the main issue was for a healing to take place. This time, however, it was needed for a paralytic so he could get up and walk. Is it easier now to understand that the main issue is always something Jesus handles?

And what were the secondary issues? Could one have been having to find Jesus? You see, Jesus didn't' come to the man, the man had to get to Jesus. Was another secondary issue determining the means by which they would get their friend inside to see Jesus? It had seemed so impossible, yet it turned out to be possible.

Was there still another secondary issue in how they were to cut the hole in the roof? And, after that, how to lower the man through the roof when the four had no rope? Did they use their imaginations? Yes! They were then able to use their sashes.

In those hard places in the lives of people, there are main issues and secondary issues. If we as stretcher-bearers support the main issues, we can concentrate fully on our primary purpose, which is to deal with the secondary issues.

WHAT OTHERS ARE SAYING

Though they have not used the term "stretcher bearers," others have also affirmed our need as Christians to care for one another. Dietrich Bonhoeffer stressed the importance of our being people who get involved in the lives of others. He described Christians as people who are meant to be persons for others.

Karl Menninger, the famed psychiatrist, knows better than most what it takes to cure the ills of the world's hurting people. And what does he prescribe for such a widespread sickness? Pills? Therapy? Not at all. The medicine he prescribes is love. Yes, it's going to take love, lots of plain ol' love that is caring, supporting and encouraging.

Teilhard de Chardin compares our harnessing the energies of love for God to some of man's obvious accomplishments in mastering the physical energies of wind, wave, tide and gravity. And he considers harnessing the energies of love for God as the greater achievement, so much so in de Chardin's opinion that he compares it to man's discovering fire for the second time in human history.

Reuben Welch, a chaplain at Point Loma College in California, wrote a book, *We Really Do Need Each Other*, in which he said:

"You know something –
we're all just people who need each other.
We're all learning
    and we've all got a long journey ahead of us.
We've got to go together
            and if it takes us until Jesus comes
    we better stay together
    we better help each other.
And I dare say
    that by the time we get there
    all the sandwiches will be gone
    and all the chocolate will be gone
    and all the water will be gone
    and all the backpacks will be empty.
But no matter how long it takes us
    we've got to go together.
    Because that's how it is
    in the body of Christ.
It's all of us
    In love
        in care
            in support
                in mutuality
                we really do need each other."[1]

CONCLUSION

Whom do you need to reach out to today? Do you hear Jesus encouraging you? Perhaps He is saying, "Come with me, for I must go to help someone who is on a stretcher. Come with me and become involved. Don't just watch me, but support me in the main issue. And, please, you deal with the secondary issues. I will still be there to give you all the insights and strengths you need, as you deal with the problems."

Think about where you might see your own involvement with others. As they begin to come into your mind, perhaps you could pray about them right now by saying, "Lord, what do I need to do to make my friends and family feel encouraged while they are on a stretcher? Show me what the secondary issues are and let me know what I can do. I need direction, Lord, on how I can reach out to them. Let me know what to say and how to act."

I have had a very special prayer for the past eight years. Every month I pray this same prayer, over and over again. My prayer has nothing to do with being a good speaker or minister whom people will respond to. It has nothing to do with becoming an author and having my book published and sold. My prayer is really a very simple prayer and I would like to share it with you:

"Lord, once again this month, make me a pair of scissors. Work through my senses so that I can get in touch with those who need their bandages removed. Lord, I just want to be a pair of scissors."

To me this is what life is all about. What about you today? Could that simple prayer become your prayer as well? Even as you read this book, pause before our Lord right now, and say, "Make me a pair of scissors. I want to remove the bandages, Lord, so I volunteer. Just show me where you want me to go with you, Lord. I want to be a pair of scissors."

Friend, this world needs scissors. What an impact you and I can have as we become scissors for Him. Remove the bandages! That is the Lord's message to you today.

PERSONAL TIME

Whose bandages does God want you to remove?

Name	*Main issues*	*Secondary issues*
A.		
B.		

GRAB A HANDLE

Are you beginning to see how important you are in the lives of others? Are people beginning to come across your mind who you know need encouragement? Grab a handle! You can do it. God bless you, stretcher-bearer!

Note

1. Taken from *We Really Do Need Each Other*, by Reuben Welch. Copyright 1976 by Impact Books, a Division of the John T. Benson Company. Copyright reassigned in 1982 to The Zondervan Corporation. Used by permission.

You get what you pay for! How often have you heard that familiar statement? We hear it repeated frequently in stores by salespeople when we are considering the purchase of such items as appliances, cars, clothing and other consumer products. I wonder if perhaps you feel as I do when they use this phrase. Sometimes I don't know if I should believe them. I find myself speculating about the possibility that the salesperson may not really know the product. I also have doubts in regard to their caring about me as a customer, thinking they just want the sale or the commission.

We may need to look more honestly at ourselves, however, as more times than not the statement "You get what you pay for," is true. When we take into consideration the quality, craftsmanship, time, effort and material, these factors all have a bearing on the cost of the item.

As we shop, we need to be both careful and aware. For instance, the same article of clothing produced by different manufacturers can look the same on the outside. But what about a few months down the road? Would we find this shirt, blouse, sweater or jacket still worth the price? The same could be said for appliances, cars and other consumer products.

Have you ever purchased an item in a store at what you were told was "a great price," only to find out later that this great price was really a great rip-off?

I remember buying a certain pair of brown shoes years ago and how I learned a lesson through the experience. I had gone shopping for shoes and found a pair that I liked a lot. But I thought they were priced too high. I remember how soft the leather felt, and when I put them on it was like walking on a cloud. I knew it would be wonderful to have this pair of shoes, but felt I should continue to shop for a less expensive pair.

I came upon another shoe store selling a shoe that looked almost identical to the higher priced pair. I was so excited! They looked just the same but they were half the price! At first, I just held the shoes. Then I put them on and walked around the store a little. I thought, "I'm going to look great in these." I could hardly believe my good fortune. What a bargain! It didn't take me very long to decide. I bought that pair of shoes, thinking I was saving nearly 50 percent.

I took the shoes home and could hardly wait until the next day when I could wear them for the first time. When morning came I was really excited. I put them on and, boy, did I look sharp! I wore them all day as well as the next day and the following day.

Two weeks went by quickly. Then something happened to the shoes. They began to crack right across the front. The smooth, soft, polished leather wasn't there any longer, and the whole front of the shoe began to buckle. My shoes now made me look like a clown.

I took the shoes back to the shoe store and was able to talk to the same salesperson. I explained that when I purchased these shoes less than a month ago, they looked fantastic. But now, within just a few weeks, they had cracked and looked terrible. I also told him I had almost bought another pair of shoes that looked just like them at another shoe store. I said that the other shoes cost twice as much but that I doubted if they would have worn as badly as these had.

The salesperson then looked at me and said something I'll not forget: "First of all, the quality of the other shoe is much higher. The leather is softer, the workmanship and craftsmanship is superb. The shoe we carry may look as good – and it is a pretty nice pair of shoes, but it can't really be compared to the shoe you were originally looking at."

He then said, "You see, you get what you pay for." There was that same statement. Now, I don't know about you, but I feel most people don't like being reminded of those familiar words. You see, I know that I would rather have had those soft leather shoes, but at half the price.

I also would like to have a new car with all the extras. But I don't necessarily want to pay for the extras. It's nice to have stylish clothes with a nice label, but I don't know if I want to pay for the label.

When we say, "The cost is way out of line," we really mean that we don't want to pay for those extras. Being human, we probably would like to have many things, but do we want to pay the full price for them?

For interest, I looked up the word cost in a dictionary. The word means "the price paid to produce, accomplish or acquire." Another definition said, "the outlay or expenditure for something." The outlay or expenditure could mean our time, money, labor and other costs.

COUNTING THE COST

Use your imagination right now to picture someone you know being on a stretcher. The reason that individual is there could be for some physical, mental, spiritual or social problem. It could possibly be some kind of a situation within his or her family. For some reason, however, this person has been placed on a stretcher.

If you wanted to be a stretcher-bearer to this friend or relative, you would find there are certain costs involved in doing this. What might it cost you to be the person who could lift that one's stretcher? List below what you think these costs might be.

1.

2.

3.

4.

5.

As you think about these costs, think also about the statement, "You get what you pay for." Could this phrase possibly apply here as you serve in stretcher bearing?

I believe it does. As I see it, you may have within your heart the desire to be a stretcher-bearer. What we need now are ways to encourage that feeling.

As you continue to read this book, I believe it can help you determine if stretcher bearing is an area where you would like to serve. One important issue you must consider, however, is your willingness to pay the cost. For you see, there are costs involved in being a stretcher-bearer. It's not the easiest of jobs and it can often be expensive to participate. You must ask yourself, "Are the costs of stretcher bearing worth the price?"

Many of these costs may not be to your liking. Yet, in stretcher bearing, some of the costs you will be considering will make you feel good, as they can be quite beautiful and very rewarding.

Yes, we need to be very honest and realize that stretcher bearing can, and often does, demand a great deal from us. To give you a better understanding, let's examine these various costs.

Our Time

If you and I are to be stretcher-bearers, one of the key costs we encounter is that of our *time*. Time is our most important asset. We all have the same amount of time. How we use it is of extreme importance. It is our most valuable asset that we distribute.

If there is one thing that seems to be in short supply, it's our time. As a result, it can be extremely difficult to share any of it. Time is so precious and it seems we always need more rather than less, yet to be a stretcher-bearer, you must find the time and share some of this precious commodity.

Through my own years of being a stretcher-bearer, I have been able to gain some valuable insights regarding the necessary division of my time. Sharing my findings I hope will help you evaluate your own ability to divide your time.

Time Schedules

When I am called upon to be that necessary stretcher-bearer, I know my *schedule* will have to be rearranged. When people are hurting I cannot look at my calendar and say, "All right, from four to five I have an opening and I can then be your stretcher bearer." Many times I must forget that such a thing as a calendar or clock even exists, as I respond to the immediate need.

You cannot schedule this ministry to your own convenience. Being a stretcher-bearer cannot happen just when you want or are able. To be a true friend and a stretcher-bearer will dictate its own schedule and arrange its own timing.

I recall the many times on my day off when I have been called upon to be a stretcher-bearer. I have even had to return while on vacation because someone had a need. I cannot count the many dinner hours that have been interrupted by a phone call because a person was hurting. When somebody is having a hard moment, I believe it can be especially important to reach out and show that person that his or her life is more important than any schedule.

Time Convenience

Being a stretcher-bearer does not occur at your own convenience. For instance, I may be away on a vacation when I am notified I should return because there has been a death. Having to return isn't particularly to my liking, but I respond because that family needs me for counseling and for the funeral for their loved one.

There is not great pleasure in having my dinner hour interrupted by a telephone call, to return later to the table and find my food cold and my family already finished. But food warms up again, and the phone is an important means for me to minister to others.

Several times I've suddenly had to leave my house at late hours of the night to go to a hospital. I won't call that a terribly convenient time to go out, but that is when someone happened to need me. That late hour of night also might be when someone will need you.

These inconvenient minutes or hours are never given in bitterness or anger because they are tender, sweet moments, and the spirit of God has opportunity to speak to you. Somehow there is a voice within you saying, "Someone needs you, someone needs you to bring the love of Christ into his or her life right now. They are hurting and they need a stretcher bearer." You know the moment then has come, and you are able to be the needed stretcher-bearer. At such times, you realize that your own personal inconvenience really was not all that much and was well worth the cost.

Since time must be counted cost in order for you to be a stretcher bearer, it could very well turn out to be a continual or long-reaching cost. As an example, your hospital visit may not take just five minutes. You might find that you have to give hours being with a person or a family. You may even have to stay up all night and be right there beside someone.

I remember a dear family that was going through a very difficult time when one of their loved ones was in critical condition and in intensive care. She was not only in a deep coma, but was suffering many seizures as well. Throughout this tough ordeal, I could really feel within myself just how much the family needed someone else to be there.

I know I couldn't' make the seizures go away and I couldn't' wake her up from the coma; these were main issues that Jesus had to deal with. But, I did know I could really become a part of the secondary issues. I could hold a hand or cry with someone. I could be a shoulder to lean on and I could give a hug. I could also join in standing by her bedside and help in making sure she did not bite her tongue when a seizure did occur.

This family needed to see and feel that all the proper care was there, not only from the doctors and nurses, but from others as well. The loving care being given to this special lady in their lives helped the family to cope.

This was a time for me that had not been set up by a previous appointment. It was also inconvenient if one wanted to look at it in that way, and it was long lasting. It continued from around nine o'clock at night until about two o'clock in the morning. Time marched by very slowly, very methodically and we were all very tired. But being a stretcher-bearer meant that I was there and I saw it through. It's true that these were all at a cost to me, but as I knew and understood what I was doing, these costs were really not very much.

If you are to be a stretcher-bearer, you must plan on it taking up your time. In analyzing yourself, are you a person who is always prompt? Are you quite good at keeping appointments and staying on top of your busy schedule? To be involved as a stretcher-bearer usually means that those schedules have to be rearranged. It can also demand that you must be somewhere for a long duration of time that may continue for hours or even days.

Earlier, you were asked to imagine someone you know being on a stretcher. We now need to think deeply about that friend or relative. You might even think about a time when you might be on a stretcher. As we think about these people, we can better understand the true value that is involved in this ministry. We can realize with fuller meaning what it would mean in having a friend who would take time to be with you.

Our Effort

As we continue to count the costs of stretcher bearing, we must consider another cost. That cost is called *effort*. After all, it is not an easy task to lift a full-laden stretcher. Not only does it take time, but it also takes strength, emotional involvement and a genuine effort. Yet, effort plus energy equals results.

Think again of the four men who carried their paralyzed friend to Jesus. Did it take an effort on their part to lift their friend and carry him? Remember how they walked up and down those dusty hot roads until they found the right home where Jesus was teaching?

Did it take an effort to figure out how to get their friend inside to see Jesus? And how about the effort involved in making a hole in the roof with the hot sun on their backs as they were cutting and digging? And finally, after they created a hole large enough for the task, what of the effort it took to lower their friend through to where Jesus stood? Then and only then were they able to see the results of their efforts.

You can never make it as a stretcher-bearer without putting effort into the job. Even as you write a letter of encouragement to someone, it still takes effort to stop and think of the special words that can minister in just the right way. If you need to visit a person in a hospital, it takes not only time, but an effort is involved just to drive through the traffic to get there. It may mean going clear across town somewhere, after which you need to find a parking place. When you visit someone in a hospital room, you can just sit there, or you can make an effort to hold their hand and pray for them.

Yes, stretcher bearing does take an effort and we can't get around that fact. It definitely takes our personal involvement; it is something that we intentionally must do.

Because of our efforts, we can become emotionally drained and then it takes additional effort to find the strength not to give up. Those men who carried their friend committed their time, their energies and their emotions, as well as their muscles and their brains.

Can you imagine how these men felt when they saw their friend walk and then pick up and carry his own stretcher out of that room? It makes you want to have been there. It had to have been worth all the effort, every single moment of it.

You can have the same kind of joyful experience after giving your best so a friend could be lifted off a stretcher. What a blessing to see the results of your effort materialize and to know that when your friend truly needed your help, you were there.

GIVING OF YOURSELF

As you buy into the concept of being a stretcher-bearer, you are going to notice something very quickly. It will become quite evident that to be a stretcher-bearer means you must give of yourself. This simply means that many things which are rightfully yours and which you have earned must be willingly given to someone else. What's more, this giving away may have to be done on just a moment's notice.

What are some of the things you might have to give up? Could time be an obvious one? We have just talked about its costs. We must not only look at the cost of our time, but we must also be prepared to give up our time. Examples would be the days off that you're entitled to, the rest you're entitled to, the vacations you're entitled to – suddenly, someone else needs these moments from you and you are called upon to give them.

Another way you give of yourself is through your energy, through your physical strength, through your own "blood, sweat and tears." Sometimes when you are a stretcher-bearer the anxiety can be draining and you may find you are very, very tired. Yet you must give up sleep. All these things that could be used for your best interests are now being given to others.

There is also the possibility of your own money being needed for someone else. That is frequently part of the giving of ourselves. When Nicole was in the hospital, we had all those bills to pay and many people donated money. They had earned this money and it was rightfully theirs. It was probably needed within their own homes to pay their own bills; to save for their own vacations, retirement and future; to buy all the things they would enjoy in life. Many people, however, willingly gave of themselves and their money so they could help our family when we were on stretchers.

Those men who carried their friend on the stretcher; how were they able to give of themselves? Hopefully, some of the means are becoming obvious. For instance, their time: It may have taken hours of walking before they found the right home. Their sashes: When they had needed a means of lowering that stretcher, they took off their sashes that were wrapped around their waists and gave them.

You always have to give of yourself when you help someone. As our prime example, we can study Jesus Christ and his relationship to us. Wasn't He a person who always gave? He was not demanding of others; He was always giving. He said that, "It is more blessed to give than to receive" (Acts 20:35). That means to give of yourself, to give personally. Jesus Christ, the greatest of all givers, came to earth so that you and I might be reconciled to God by the gift of Himself.

Giving of yourself. It is a cost. But when seen through the eyes of a stretcher-bearer, is it really too high a price to pay?

BECOMING EMOTIONALLY INVOLVED

As you become a stretcher-bearer, your own emotions or feelings cannot help but become involved. You cannot involve yourself and leave your emotions uninvolved, because as a stretcher-bearer, everything about you will become totally dedicated to what you are doing.

As you get close to people and lift their stretchers, you will often see them cry in their pain and hurt. This hurt can come for a variety of reasons, including the experience of death. You will probably become very aware then of emotional feelings going on within yourself. It's terribly hard to see someone hurt or cry and know that you cannot make that hurt go away or stop the tears.

To be present in a room when someone's loved one died brings the realization that this experience is final and you cannot bring that precious person back. Suddenly your emotions react. Yes, there will be those times when being a stretcher bearer can really get to you.

Paul told us to "carry each other's burdens" (Gal. 6:2). As we do this, however, we cannot help but feel what others are feeling. You may not hurt to the degree of intensity as the person who is on the stretcher, but more times than not you will be hurting right along with that one.

You will be with a family and will want to be their encourager and their person of strength, and you will find yourself crying right along with them. Many times the handkerchief you brought along to wipe away tears from the eyes of others is wiping away your own tears. Stretcher bearing touches upon your own emotional feelings.

Don't be ashamed of these feelings and don't think you are inadequate to serve as a stretcher-bearer. There can be times when others need to see someone else cry with them. I believe someone on a stretcher has a need to feel somebody else hurts almost as deeply as they do. I have learned in these years of being a stretcher-bearer that it is alright to cry and let my emotional involvement show.

A stretcher-bearer needs to be real. When people see that we are not only involved and want to help, but that we are real and our emotions are showing, it is easier for them to accept us. By and through this acceptance they can unburden themselves somewhat through talking out their grief more openly. They also will be thankful to you for being yourself and for being a real friend.

Emotional Rejection

A totally different type of emotional experience can also happen to you. It may occur at a time when you know someone truly is in need of help. You want to be able to reach out to them because you know they are drowning, but they reject you. To feel this type of rejection will drain you emotionally and also give you a feeling of frustration. Many times it is so obvious that someone is on a stretcher; but still they refuse our help. They simply say, "Leave me alone. I don't need your help."

There isn't anyone who likes rejection. I know I would rather hear, "Thanks for being there, thanks for caring." To sense someone needs help and hear him or her say, "I don't need you" can hurt. It especially hurts when it is so obvious that person is drowning. Yet this is part of the cost that is involved in being a stretcher-bearer.

There will be times when tears and emotions are shared together, and there will be other times when you are emotionally drained because someone rejected your assistance. All you can do is pray for that person in a special way and remember to be open to them if they should ever indicate they need your help. Don't feel that you have failed them. This is just something that happens within the lives of certain people.

Emotional Helplessness

Feeling helpless in a crisis situation can leave you emotionally drained. Inevitably, you will go through times when you feel bound in helplessness. In certain situations where someone is on a stretcher needing your support, the situation itself may be something you are unable to be a part of. You feel as though your hands are tied. There is nothing you can do.

For example, a friend or relative is going through a divorce and is not the one in the marriage who wanted the divorce. You would love to help patch up that marriage, but you can't. It is left as an issue between that husband and wife and their lawyers. You know you can pray, but you also find yourself wishing there was something else you could do.

Another example is when someone you know may be having a financial crisis. Your friend may need $5,000. How you would love to have $5,000 to give that friend but all you have is $100. There again is that feeling of helplessness and it can tax you emotionally. The anxiety within yourself often increases, as you look and wish for ways to help your friend off that stretcher.

The advice? Do what you can do. As a stretcher-bearer that is all you are called to do. Take into consideration that there are many circumstances where you simply could not do something all by yourself. The Mark 2 story showed the need for four people. You may find yourself wishing there were three more to join you but maybe there isn't anyone else.

You must realize when these times come; you can only do your part. Your part is all God calls you to do. Keep stretcher bearing and your emotions in the proper perspective. Try to realize that we can't do it all. We can only do what we can. That is all God calls us to do.

RISKING YOURSELF

To be a stretcher-bearer involves risking yourself. To risk means you are going to take a chance on what you feel and sense and what you believe God is saying to you regarding the help another person needs. What you risk is your position of being comfortable where you are, without involvement and without cost to yourself.

Once a month in our church, we write letters of encouragement to one another. We take the time to do this during our Sunday morning church service. On page 164, I describe this whole concept in greater detail.

Basically, the congregation is furnished a specially designed postcard. Then about 300 people take the time to write a note on the cards to someone whom they believe God has put upon their minds, someone they sense might need a word of encouragement or comfort. During the service we allow about five minutes to write these cards. They are then collected along with the morning offering. On Monday morning the office staff and volunteers look up addresses, stamp and mail the cards.

During that morning church service, 300 people believe that God has placed a certain person into their thoughts. Everyone may not sense the exact leading of the Spirit, but what they do feel is an awareness inside toward a person and they want to risk themselves by encouraging this person. What they are risking is their position of being non involved. Instead they are saying, "I am going to take a chance."

When those cards are received and read, they have proved to be a real blessing for many who have needed such encouragement just when the cards arrived.

To sit back and not become involved in another's life is simple, easy and safe. But then no one is helped. The one who dares to risk himself or herself is the one who will possibly save someone else from drowning.

It took an effort on my part to save the young boy from drowning at Huntington Beach. In fact, it took a great deal of effort to swim through the water and then try to get us both back to shore. There was a cost involved. After all, this young man, Steve, was not crying out for help. What if I had waited for him? He might have called too late or not called at all. I had to go by the feelings going on inside me that said, "Go! Go right now! Take the chance, risk yourself, maybe he's all right and maybe you'll be embarrassed, but embarrassment can wear off. To drown would be much too costly."

I listened to these inner feelings and I saved someone's life. It proved to be not only worth the risk, but it proved to be extremely profitable. Profitable not only for me, but also for Steve.

When you reach out, many times you will hear people say, "Thank you, thank you for taking the chance and caring for me."

Other times you may not hear any particular response. But that's okay, keep right on trying. It's like being a baseball player; you must keep swinging the bat. Sooner or later you are bound to make contact with the ball. If you keep the bat on your shoulder or you never get out of the dugout, you'll never even get a base hit. Keep swinging!

That's what makes a baseball player like Reggie Jackson so exciting to watch. He strikes out many times, but when he strikes out, he always goes out swinging. And other times he doesn't strike out – he gets that hit. Over 500 times in his career, he has hit a home run. The reason? He goes up to home plate, he risks himself, he swings and when he hits that ball – it was worth the risk.

May we be just as intense in being stretcher-bearers as Reggie Jackson is in playing baseball. Let's risk ourselves and swing. Let's give it all the effort we can. More times than not, we will at least make a base hit and sometimes we'll even get that home run. What a moment each one can be!

BEING CREATIVE

Creativity is an exciting part of the total stretcher bearing cost. The reason it's exciting is because creativity allows us to use our imagination. As our imagination widens, we are able to find ways in which we can help other people.

Use your imagination now. Picture or think about people you know who are on stretchers. Through your own creativity, how can you show that you want to be their stretcher-bearer? Perhaps a person you know is feeling lonely. Could you invite that person for dinner? Or the young boy next door can't afford to go to a football game and you know he loves football. Can you buy him a ticket or take him?

I personally know a young boy who doesn't have a father. I also know he loves playing Little League baseball. One day I thought, "Why don't I get some tickets to a major league base-ball game and I'll take him."

Friends, that's just what I did. We saw the game, ate hot dogs and had a great time together.

This young fellow continued playing Little League baseball. One day, he was talking to me about a very special baseball bat he had seen. He just knew he could hit a home run with it. Later, I was talking to my wife about this and I said, "Tony can't afford a baseball bat right now because of the situation in his family. Do you think you and I could buy him that bat?" We did. It really didn't cost us very much and we gave it to him as a gift.

This would be called using our creativity. We use our imagi-nation to help someone who was on a "little stretcher." To Tony, this was a "little stretcher" time. The lack of funds so he could buy a baseball bat was discouraging to him. And I thought it was a little tough for him to see friends he knew having special baseball bats.

I know it brought us pleasure to buy him the bat, and a few weeks later, guess what? He hit that home run with it. He was so excited. He came to me and told me, "I hit a home run with the bat you bought me!" Tony and I became even closer because of this involvement.

Yes, creativity can enable us to be persons of encouragement and support. In other words, stretcher-bearers.

Because the story presents so many facets of the whole con-cept of stretcher bearing, we return again to the account of the four men who carried their friend on a stretcher to see Jesus. Notice how creatively these men used their imaginations. They were creative when they chose to reach Jesus by going through the roof after finding their way to the door blocked by crowds.

Reaching the roof and lacking proper tools for the job, they creatively made use of their knives to open up the roof. The same creativity led them to use their sashes in lieu of ropes, so they could lower their friend down through the hole to Jesus.

Creative imagination – that's all it takes. And the Lord has gifted us with imagination. Pray for wisdom in finding creative and imaginative ways that will allow you to enter someone's life and minister to that person as a stretcher bearer.

DANGER POINTS

The purpose of stretcher bearing is to help another person in some way. The objective is to support and encourage this person so he or she can later live a life that is fulfilling and worthwhile. Such support is meant to give them renewed strength and a new outlook. Then, when that person is lifted off the stretcher, he or she will be able to continue on with a new lease on life.

Sometimes, however, a problem area arises. On several occasions when I reached out to be a stretcher-bearer, I found those persons needed me as a crutch as well. In other words, they had become dependent on me. They were refusing to get off their stretchers even though they were capable of doing so.

I found that this type of problem often arises when I'm counseling. I discovered it is more pronounced in couples that are going through marital difficulties. Therefore, I am aware of this potential danger point whenever I counsel. I am even more alert when I am involved in encouraging a married couple in ways that will strengthen their marriage.

If I am seeing a couple month after month, it becomes apparent to me when they are not doing the things they know they should do. Then, when their marriage is once again rocky, back they come to my office saying, "Pastor Mike will help. He'll help us get our marriage back where it should be."

This particular cycle, unfortunately, can go on and on. The reason they are in trouble, however, is clear; they are still refusing to do what they are capable of doing.

When you, as a stretcher-bearer, become involved in another person's life and problems, be aware of people who are becoming too dependent. You need to realize that this could be a possible danger point for you.

You will be able to tell when they are too dependent, because they refuse to get off their stretcher. Another way to phrase this is to say that they refuse to learn to swim. After rescuing them repeatedly, you feel they should want to learn to swim, so they would not be in danger of drowning again. Then you will have the feeling that they are able to handle their hard situations without you.

Reflect upon the boy named Steve whom I saved from drowning at Huntington Beach. I not only needed to help Steve so he wouldn't drown, but I needed to get the message across to him, "You not only have to learn how to swim, you have to learn how to call for help when you need it.

"The key, Steve, is not in the calling for help, the key is to know what to do before you need help. You need to recognize signs, such as being tired, long before you feel the current taking you out farther and farther. You need to learn, Steve, which way to swim, so you can avoid those currents and be able to make it safely to shore."

As a stretcher-bearer, you are not just to encourage people, but encourage them in such a way that they are capable of living their life without your assistance anymore.

As you become involved in counseling people, you need to instruct them as you reach out. Teach them, as you watch them recover from their illnesses, heartbreaks and emotional situations. You need to continue to be a stretcher-bearer, but be careful of the danger in becoming a crutch.

We know that Jesus is that mighty strength and force which is a power within us, and we need to rely upon Him. But, we should never see Jesus as a crutch!

There are many people who think Christianity itself is a crutch. This is unfortunate and another danger point, as Christianity is not a crutch. It's a working relationship with a powerful God, and we need to continually work at that relationship.

We need to incorporate that power, plus the ministry of the Holy Spirit, within our lives. God isn't going to do our work for us. Rather, we need to work with Him. It isn't God who is going to make your marriage strong – it is you who must make your marriage strong – through Christ.

God isn't going to make you a success in business just because you think He should. Being a success happens only when you let Christ work His principles through you and within you.

This is the whole concept of working with God. We cannot just expect that God will do it for us. We use this same concept within the ministry of stretcher bearing. We cannot allow people to just expect us to do everything for them. Yet we need to continue to work with others – within their lives. We in turn need to allow them to work with us – within our lives.

What we need to be aware of are the danger points, and we need to be careful not to "run" another's life. We cannot become a crutch where we need continually to be there. We need to help them when they need help, but at the same time, we must encourage them to learn to swim.

FEELING WORTHWHILE

Many people who are walking around today feel as though their lives serve no purpose or have no worth. They actually feel that if they should die tomorrow – no big deal! The world will still go on and they will not even be missed. Life will go on as though they had never existed.

I remember growing up among our high school youth group, and the youth minister told us the following: "You know, each of you is but a grain of sand. A grain of sand on the beach. Have you ever gone to a beach, put your towel down on the sand, and after staying a while, picked up your towel and gone home from the beach? As you shook out your towel, many grains of sand fell to the floor. Do you think any of those grains of sand would be missed from the beach?"

We all thought about this and decided, "No, there is plenty of sand down there and no one would ever know that they are missing."

He then answered us by saying, "That's how it is with your life. If you die tomorrow, Christianity and the Church will still go on. They are not dependent on you."

A grain of sand? This was not the best epitaph to one's life. The reason I get so excited about the concept of being a stretcher-bearer is, because I don't feel his analysis is correct. It's also probably why I feel it is important to encourage others to be stretcher-bearers.

I know that as you become a stretcher-bearer, you are much more than a grain of sand. You are a part of creation and involved in this world. You, therefore, must be involved within the lives of other people. They, too, are a part of creation and God dearly loves us all. Being a stretcher-bearer says, "My life can count. My life can count a great deal because I know I am needed to help another person."

You and I need to know that we are definitely more than mere numbers. We are more than just persons on this earth. Your life has meaning. My life has meaning and there are people who need us today. Other lives can be touched through our lives.

You and I have the ability to be that type of special friend mentioned in Proverbs 18:24, *TLB*. Then people could quote that verse and say, "There are friends that pretend to be a friend, yet there is a friend that stands closer than a brother." Yes, you and I can be that kind of friend.

Stretcher bearing has allowed me to have a sense of purpose for myself and in the ministry God has called me to. I cannot even count how many phone calls and letters I have received saying, "Thank you." Or how many people have come up to me and said, "Thank you for being a part of my life when I needed someone." My friends, I honestly must share with you how good these comments make me feel inside. These expressions of love and gratitude are what make me want to continue this ministry.

Today I know that I am much more than a grain of sand. There is a purpose for Mike Slater. My purpose is to have a ministry within the lives of people. This is what gives me a sense of worth – the ability to say with determination that my life can count for my Lord Jesus Christ and for others. Your life counts, too, because you are worthwhile. To become a stretcher-bearer will only enhance your self-worth and enlarge upon the purposes you have in life.

TIME IN PRAYER

When you become a stretcher-bearer you will find yourself needing earnestly to talk with God. This will have to be counted as a cost, however, since you will be spending more time in prayer. It is a cost that is of real benefit to you, because this intimate time of prayer will develop a bond between you and the Lord.

Your relationship with Him will become more and more significant. You will find yourself completely open to love and care for the same people God dearly loves and cares for. The result is magnetic, and you and God are drawn closer together. You will have a continuing sense of feeling good about your relationship with Him. You will also feel reassured about your personal call into this ministry, which in turn will encourage you to continue to pray.

There is no doubt that stretcher bearing creates a bond between you and God. The time you spend meditating and being in prayer about people who are in your heart is a time well spent, because the reward is a stronger relationship with the Lord.

BROTHERLY LOVE

Through the ministry of stretcher-bearers, I have truly learned what it means to be a brother or sister in Jesus Christ. It is so easy just to say those two words, "brother" or "sister." But what we need to do is understand and live out the true meaning and concept of those words. This, at times, can be very difficult.

It is easy to sing the song, "They Will Know We Are Christians by Our Love," and it is easy to tell others, "We are a family, a family of believers in Jesus Christ." Yet, to live out in a meaningful way what we are saying, takes true effort.

Being a stretcher-bearer created for me new and stronger friendships. We are bonded together in a family intimacy. I don't personally believe anyone or anything else could have created this same closeness.

When a person's life is really touched, when you and others know that you really care for one another, most people never forget the experience. The reason for this is because a bond is created between yourself and the other person. It is so solidly locked with Jesus Christ, that this bond always remains.

If a time should ever come for you to be on a stretcher, usually it's the people you have reached out to who reach out to you. This type of love assures you that you will never walk alone in this world. You will always have that brother or sister to be a companion and friend.

CELEBRATION

By now you know what costs are involved in being a stretcher-bearer. And some of these costs are quite demanding. But costs that return more to a person than were put in are, in actuality, an investment. And that return on cost expended is a dividend. Stretcher bearing can be very rewarding, enjoyable and fulfilling. And that's an enormous dividend. Investing in brotherly love always pays dividends and benefits to all concerned.

I want to tell you about another dividend on this life investment called stretcher bearing. And this dividend outweighs all the costs involved. It is called celebration.

A frequent opportunity you will have in being a stretcher-bearer is that special moment when a person is lifted off the stretcher. He or she enters into a new life of recovery, purpose and fulfillment. Such a moment is a true cause for celebration, not only for that person, but also for you, the stretcher-bearer.

Remember imagining how the four stretcher-bearing men felt when Jesus healed their crippled friend? We tried to picture their excitement as they saw him get off that stretcher and walk for the first time in many, many years. We could almost see the tears of pure joy flowing as they celebrated this victorious moment together. And the happiness of the bearers would be no less than that of their newly healed friend.

Now imagine Lazarus coming slowly out of that cave. Next see him as those bandages are removed. He begins to smile as he sees his friends and family once again.

To have taken part in that great time of celebration would be a true cause for joy and laughter. To hear the excitement, as some were able to shout, "I was part of it." "I helped roll away the stone." "I cut those bandages." "I showed Jesus where we had laid Lazarus." Friends, this was a true time of celebration, and everyone was invited to the party.

I have been able to take part in many celebrations. Perhaps you also have been able to celebrate. Our hope in the future would be for everyone to attend parties of celebration, as people are lifted from their stretchers.

One celebration I attended was with a lady I wrote about earlier. She had been in a coma having continual seizures and, through the grace of God, is walking today. I have been to her home. She is smiling today. I sat with her and watched her eat dinner. We have laughed, hugged and kissed as we celebrated this victory through Jesus Christ.

This also brings to mind the young woman, Lisa, and her difficult pregnancy. I went through those hard times with Lisa and her husband, Keith. I was at that first celebration when that sweet baby was born. Now we all continue to celebrate together as we watch this dear child developing and growing up.

SUMMARY

In this chapter, I have tried to show you an honest picture, for you needed to know that stretcher bearing is not easy. It's not always the most joyous experience, as there are many demands. There is the price of involvement, and you must be willing to pay the price. At the same time, we need to remember that there is a price to be paid to produce or accomplish anything worthwhile in life.

If we could see every cost through the eyes of Jesus, we see that they are not unjustified. They are all worth the price.

Which pair of shoes will you buy? They are not all the same, and you will get what you pay for. Do you want to be a stretcher-bearer? There are costs, and there is no shortcut around them. But since you get as much or more out of stretcher bearing as you put into it, these costs are well worth the price. In fact, they are investments, because they pay dividends in brotherly love and in personal fulfillment.

Another big dividend is celebration. I know, as I have witnessed these celebrations. They are indeed wonderful times of victory and rejoicing. And when those times come, each of us will have paid the price to deserve that celebration.

I'm sure you want to help celebrate these victories, too, and will say with me, "I am going to be a stretcher bearer and pay the cost!"

PERSONAL TIMES

Are there cost factors you need to overcome?

_____

_____

_____

GRAB A HANDLE

Explore the benefits of paying the price and overcoming cost factors and thus investing ourselves in one another.

EIGHT

It was back in chapter four that I told you about an airline that was bound for Florida that crashed. If I may, I would like to share more of the story and in particular a comment that was made at the crash site; it has had a tremendous impact upon me and my ministry of encouragement and support. Following is part of the article from *Time* Magazine.

THE JET BOUND FOR FLORIDA

Flurries of thick, wet snow swirled through the streets of Washington, clogging traffic and slowing down pedestrians to a labored trudge. As the snow piled up, government offices and private businesses closed early and sent their workers home. By mid-afternoon, traffic on the bridges over the Potomac River that link the capital with its Virginia suburbs had already slowed to a crawl. Meanwhile, Washington National Airport had just reopened after having been shut down by the snowfall for two hours. At 3:59 a flight bound for Tampa, a Bowing 737 with 74 passengers aboard began rolling down the airport's main runway for takeoff.

Lloyd Creger, an administrative assistant in the Justice Department was inching along the northbound span of the 14th Street Bridge in his Chevrolet when he heard the roar of the flight taking off for Florida. He thought nothing of it; hundreds of planes every day take off from National and head out over the bridge.

But this time it was different. Creger watched in horror as the blue and green jetliner suddenly appeared out of the gray mist. The plane slammed into the crowded bridge, smashed five cars and a truck and then skidded into the frozen river. "It was falling from the sky, coming right at me," recalls Creger. "It hit the bridge and just kept on going like a rock into the water." He remembers that the plane's nose was tilted up when its tail crashed into the bridge, as if the pilot was trying with all his strength to keep the jet aloft.

For a moment, there was silence and then pandemonium. Commuters watched helplessly as the plane quickly sank beneath the ice flows; only its tail remained visible. A few passengers bobbed to the surface; some clung numbly to pieces of debris while others screamed desperately for help. Scattered across the ice were pieces of green upholstery, twisted chunks of metal, luggage, a tennis racquet, a child's shoe. On the bridge, a red flatbed truck with a 20 foot crane swung over the water. Two of the cars were flattened like tin cans.

Within minutes sirens began to wail as fire trucks, ambulances and police cars rushed to the scene. A U.S. Park Police helicopter hovered overhead to pluck survivors out of the water. Six were clinging to the plane's tail. Dangling a life preserver ring to them, the chopper began ferrying them to shore. One woman had injured her right arm, so Pilot Don Usher lowered the copter until its skids touched the water' his partner scooped her up in his arms.

Then Priscilla Tirado, grabbed the preserver, but as she was being helped out of the icy river by fellow passenger Joseph Stiley, she lost her grip. Lenny Skutnik, a clerk for the Budget Office who was watching from the shore, plunged into the water and dragged her to land. But the most notable act of heroism was performed by one of the passengers, a balding man in his early 50's. Each time the ring was lowered, he grabbed it and passed it along to another passenger. When the helicopter finally returned to pick him up, he had disappeared beneath the ice.

Meanwhile, rescue workers feverishly tossed out ropes and ladders over the frozen river and launched rubber dinghies, but their efforts were hampered by floating chunks of ice. As dusk fell, search lights were switched on, but by 5:30 officials realized the quest was in vain.

Divers sent down to inspect the fuselage has discovered that nearly all of the passengers were strapped in their seats The toll; 70 dead, including four motorists. Only five aboard the airplane, four passengers and a stewardess survived the airline crash.

One possible cause of the crash was that the plane's engines may have sucked up slush from the runway, thereby diminishing their power during the critical climb at takeoff. Survivor Joseph Stiley is a pilot and he recalls that "the plane was just too heavy as it was going down the runway." He remembers turning to his friend in the next seat – who also survived the crash – and saying, "We're not going to make it."

WE'RE NOT GOING TO MAKE IT

When I read the account of the crash, I remember, putting down the magazine and began to think about the article. As I did I was captured by the phrase that Joseph Stiley had said to his friend. "We're not going to make it." I could not get that phrase and thought out of my mind. To hear those words spoken and then, within moments, to become part of that phrase. The people in the water, holding onto whatever was afloat, the people on the shore; watching, yelling encouraging words, what might be going through their minds?

It was then that I realized that phrase or thought is exactly what so many people feel in regards to situations, circumstances that occur during life; I'm not going to make it." It may not even be a phrase that sounds so desperate. It could be a statement that bellows frustration. Phrases like I cannot take it. How much longer? Why does God not answer my prayer? Why is this happening to me and my family? It's not fair! It's hopeless. Why me? I am at the end of my rope. I do not know what else I can do.

I began to recall the cry of so many people that I have encountered during my life as a minister. Listening to stories of situations that seem to be unable to be solved, challenges that they must face: health, finances, divorce, loss of a loved one, marriage. Hearing from those who are alone, scared, on the edge, fearful of what the future might bring. Their dreams shattered, their lives upturned; not in control of their own destiny. The people and the stories are so many in number.

TIME FOR US TO SHOUT

As I began to think about so many people that evening that were feeling like they were not going to make it, a powerful thought came to my mind. When people do feel like they are not going to make it, our job or ministry is to shout louder, *WE'RE GOING TO MAKE IT.*"

I thought this to be so true and needed. We need to come alongside of hurting people with our voice and efforts; encouraging, lifting and offering help.

There is a perfect portion of scripture that speaks so clearly to the hurting and their need for someone to come alongside of them to offer help and encouragement. In Ecclesiastes 4:9-12 it reads "Two are better than one because they have a good return for their work: If one falls down, his friend can help him up. But pity the man who falls and has no one to help him up! Also, if two lie down together, they will keep warm,. But how can one keep warm alone? Though one may be overpowered, two can defend themselves. A cord of three strands is not quickly broken."

I believe what the writer is trying to say is that there will be times in life that will be pretty tough. Life situations can trip you up and you fall. It could be of your own doing or sometimes the unexpected will come your way and offer you challenges. The writer states he does not feel sorry for you that you are faced with this challenge, he does say "I pity that you have fallen and no one is there to help you up." What is so interesting to me is the word pity. Pity is a word that describes a deep feeling towards someone that is beyond feeling sorry for them.

He goes on further to say that there are times in life that can be extremely cold. Once again the reason is not stated, only that the person is going through it. He asks, how can one keep warm when you are shivering and freezing within? You can squeeze yourself, but to no avail.

What is needed during this time is for someone beside to come alongside of you with a warm touch of encouragement, support and their presence. He states that in life, two are better than one. Though one may be overpowered, put two of us together and there is a strength beyond one. Put three of us together and there is a cord of three strands that is not quickly broken.

So simply and clearly stated life brings to us challenges to be faced, making us ask the question if and how are we going to make it. Needing that someone to come alongside of us to lift and encourage , offering strength, determination, resources, hope; a stretcher bearer. A stretcher bearer shouting "we are going to make it."

SOME STORIES OF SHOUTING

I remember a past occurrence that involved a woman from my church. She was having some medical issues that suggested cancer and possible surgery. I had been informed as to when she would be seen by the doctor to review her test results. I made sure to be there that particular day.

When I arrived, I went to the receptionist to ask if she and her husband had arrived. I was told that they had and were in consultation at that moment. She asked if I was a family member. I responded with a no "I'm her minister." She told me that it would be another 20 minutes before they were to come out from the doctor's office. She suggested that I take a seat. I found a vacant chair and began to read one of the outdated magazines that are always present in a doctor's office.

After sitting there a few minutes, I had a strong feeling that I was being stared at. I looked up from the magazine to see that the receptionist had walked up to me. She then asked me the following question: "Why are you here?" Every week we see 30 or more patients with medical issues; questions that must be answered, procedures that may be required. I cannot recall a minister, priest, rabbi ever sitting in this office to offer support to a patient and I am sure many have a church or a place of worship that they attend. What makes you so different?

I looked at her and said, "there are many times in life people are faced with challenges and difficult times. Times when they wonder if they are going to make it. This is such a time for this wife and husband. I am just coming alongside of them to encourage and let them know that they are going to make it. I cannot read the results of the tests or do the surgery. But, I can be by their side and help with my presence and prayers. I hope that will be a strength to them at this time."

She looked at me and after a moment a few tears came down her cheek. The look on her face and tears impacted me as I was sitting there. She then spoke these moving words, "Can you tell me about your church. I can use a church like that in my life."

A few moments after our conversation the door opened from the examining room and the wife and her husband walked out. His eyes caught mine and he walked over to me. We shook hands and he proceeded to tell me the following. "Everything is going to be alright Pastor Mike. We are so thankful. I want you to know how I felt when I opened the door and I saw you there seated waiting for us. I will never forget this time and the picture that is in my mind. I make you a promise. When people are on that side of the door and I know about it, I will be there for them. No one should experience times like that alone."

I reached out gave him a hug and said, "way to go!" When people feel like they are not going to make it, let us just shout a little louder, we are going to make it. Our voices and presence can make a difference in lives and the challenges that many are facing.

A LITTLE LEAGUE BASEBALL GAME

The other summer I went to see someone play in a little league baseball game from my church. It was a warm summer afternoon and I found myself watching the game from along the fence on the first base side. This is a better position to watch the game then from the stands. You are closer to the field, able to see the action and hear the words that are spoken.

As I was watching the game there was this player from the opposing team who was playing right field. Now, you have to remember this is little league. Young children between 6-8. Their skills are still being developed and their attention span to the game is something less than can be desired. Well this player in right field for the first three innings missed every ball that came his way. It did not matter if it was a fly ball, he would drop it. If it was a grounder that came his way it would go through his legs. The young man was truly having a difficult time at his position.

In the fourth inning a fly ball was hit towards him. He got under it, put out his glove and missed making the catch. He went back to his position, stood there with his head in his chest. The manager of the team, a father, saw the young man and asked for a time out. He left the dugout and walked to right field towards this 6 year old. I was standing by the fence and heard and witnessed the following.

The manager stopped right in front of the young boy. He then spoke the following words. "Mr. Smith, Mr. Smith. I need to inform you that one cannot catch a ball hit to you if your head is in your chest. You have to look up and be prepared. Your head in your chest is not the position to catch a ball. Now, Mr. Smith, you need to lift your head up and get prepared to play. If I did not believe in you Mr. Smith, you would not be playing this position. Now no one catches all the balls hit to them. But you will catch more if your head is up. Do you understand me Mr. Smith?"

The young boy nodded his head and the manager proceeded to return to the dugout. Now this is a true story. The next batter hit a ball out to right field towards Mr. Smith. Sometimes in life one does not need much time to pray for someone in need. I quickly looked up and said "Lord if you ever did a miracle let it be now and allow this young man to catch a ball.

Mr. Smith got under the ball, stuck out his glove, closed his eyes and held his mitt up high. After a moment, he looked down to the ground, since that was where every ball seemed to land that was hit to him. He looked around and could not find it. He then looked in his mitt and to his surprise the ball was positioned perfect and he had made the catch. He took the ball out of his glove and held it up high and then threw it back in. The manager from the dugout shouted, "way to go Mr. Smith . Keep your head up and you will catch baseballs. Mr. Smith had the biggest smile on his face.

I AM BUYING STOCK IN YOU

I recall a conference in the mountains when I was just starting out in my ministry, that had a tremendous impact upon my thinking, my ministry and self worth. Attending a youth conference as a young youth minister, I was in awe of some of the other ministers present. Men and women whom I respected and were inspirations to me and my ministry.

One afternoon one of these ministers came up to me and said, "I would love the privilege of getting together with you Mike. How about over a coke this evening after I get done speaking?

I could not believe what I just heard. This successful, highly regarded minister wanted to sit down with me and talk. Why? I felt both honored and frightened. Why would he want to take the time and spend it with a young youth minister?

That evening we did get together over cokes and had a great time getting to know one another. I cannot recall all that this man shared with me, but I do remember one statement he made that has stayed with me as a real source of encouragement.

As our conversation came to a close he looked me straight into my eyes and said, "Michael, I want to tell you something. This evening I am buying stock in you as a person and as a young youth minister. Right now, as you begin your ministry, the stock is not at a high. But one day , stock in you is going to pay big dividends. I am buying into it right now because I believe in you and your response to the plan God has for your life."

Here was a man with years of successful ministry , not yet knowing me closely, yet willing, not only to sit down and have a coke with me, but also willing to risk himself with words and thoughts of encouragement. He said, I believe in you right now as you begin, even as you experiment and as you grow toward being the man the Lord intends you to be."

That evening as I walked alone among the pines, I prayed, "Lord, what is this all about? What can the words of this good man mean. Were they words from you. Were they the inspiration and encouragement you know I needed to hear? Will the stock pay off and will there be dividends years down the road?"

Over and over in my mind I kept hearing the phrase, "I'm buying stock in you now and one day it is going to pay big dividends…I'm buying stock in you."

If you ask me how many times over the next few years that man gave me a call, I could not tell you. If you ask me how many letters and words of encouragement I received , I do not know. The lunches and time spent together over the years were numerous.

A few years ago this man died and went to be with the Lord. I gave his wife a call one afternoon and asked if I could pay her a visit. She said she would appreciate that. The following day I went to visit her and found myself sitting at her kitchen table enjoying a piece of cake. She was a great cook and baker. It was during our conversation that I told her I would like to tell her a personal story about her husband and me.

I proceeded to tell her the story lived out many years ago at the conference. I got to the part where I was gong to tell her what her husband had said to me, when she suddenly stopped me from talking. She looked at me with the most tender and peaceful eyes and said, "I know what you are gong to say. You were going to say that my husband bought stock in you that evening. Were you not?" I shook my head with a tear in my eye. She said, "Michael, I know that story because my husband shared it with me. He believed in you Michael. He told me, 'honey, God has his hands on that young minister.' He also told me years later, 'honey, the stock is paying off.'"

Now, years later this incident, along with many others brings to my mind the realization that God placed certain people into my life to be a source of encouragement and support both in my ministry and my personal life. I call them stretcher-bearers, those encouragers and supporters God uses in the lives of others. Those people who shout louder, as they come alongside, *"WE ARE GOING TO MAKE IT."*

"I KILLED MY SON"

There are times that we simply don't know what to do for family members or friends on the stretchers of life during a Gethsemane moment. The sheer pain and terror of confronting that pain immobilizes us.

A fellow stretcher-bearer and friend, Bob Hunt, told me of the time he received a phone call to go to a local hospital because of a horrible accident involving a close friend. The caller, so stunned, couldn't talk except to repeat the name of the hospital and the person involved in the accident.

Bob, unaware of the specifics of the accident, rushed to the emergency room, only to be confronted by blank stares and hysterical sobbing.

"What happened?" Bob pleaded with someone he knew in the waiting room to give him some understanding of the situation.

"Chris wants to see you," was the only reply. A split second later, Bob and his good friend came eye to eye.

"As long as I live I'll never forget that moment," Bob recalled to me, looking away to some distant spot.

"Chris looked me straight in the eye, and with a look of mixed horror and pain I have never seen since, said to me, 'Bob, I just killed my son.'"

Bob learned how his friend had tragically backed over his infant son with his car. The baby boy would die in the emergency room.

"There was nothing I could say. No words, no prayers, nothing. We just looked at each other for what seemed like an eternity."

In that moment Bob did the only thing he could do; be there for a friend. He held his friend Chris close as they embraced in silence, while the commotion of the emergency room stirred around them. In the middle of tragedy, we often wish we could say the right thing, or pray the anointed prayer. But sometimes, we are best to be silent, and simply listen.

Bob recalled how he, for months after the tragedy, would walk with his friend. The conversations ranged from the mundane to the philosophical; sometimes shattered by Chris saying to himself, "I killed my son." Again, there was never a wise follow-up answer or profound prayer, just a silent acknowledgement and listening ear.

I believe that those walks were critical to Chris' healing process. They were Bob's way of bringing his friend to the feet of Jesus.

I READ YOUR LETTER

One of the "secrets" of stretcher-bearing is understanding the beauty of many simple acts of encouragement and support.

The saying goes, "People don't care how much you know until they know how much you care."

You don't have to be a theologian or evangelist to share the Good News. People desperately want to be noticed and cared about. And, it's usually the simple act of kindness that leaves the most profound memories.

As a pastor, I've always encouraged my staff to lift stretchers with the little things available in life. One of the easiest ways is to write a note or letter of encouragement. One young inexperienced youth pastor wrote letters systematically to all the youth as a part of his job. He kept a careful file making sure that eventually everyone would receive one. He found some letters easier to write than others. Often the kids in his youth group who seemed discouraged, or on the fringe, received more attention than the others.

One teen, who was an extremely popular, athletic, blond, surfer kid, was due a letter. Because this youth pastor was only a couple of years older than the teen, he was intimidated by his "Greek god" status. Dutifully, yet with some trepidation, he wrote the young man, Brent, a letter of encouragement.

I believe the Holy Spirit uses us at times like this in ways we may never know until eternity. We write words from thoughts that we rightfully believe are our own. I'm convinced that this is where the Holy Spirit often does His work.

My youth pastor finished his letter to Brent, applied the stamp, and mailed it. But, it would be years later until he would learn of its impact.

Brent, now a young man, walked into the Bible study being held at a home. He still had the kind of striking good looks that catch the notice of men and women alike. Because a few years had passed, he reintroduced himself to my former youth pastor who was leading the study.

"Remember me?" Before he could respond, Brent reverently pulled out of his wallet a letter. "I read this everyday," Brent said looking at the well-worn paper. "It gives me hope when I'm discouraged." Brent carefully folded it back into his wallet.

Then Brent said something that stunned all those listening around him.

"I've wanted to kill myself many times." He said it in a bold way, as if to ward off any pity.

"But, every time I've tried, I read your letter."

We never know how the Holy Spirit will use us. We just have to be willing to be used.

WE ARE CALLED TO MINISTER

We are called to minister. I truly believe that one of our purposes in life is to come alongside of people to encourage, lift, assist and help in someway. When your eyes are focused on Jesus, you awaken to the fact that faith and trust in Christ makes you want to be involved in the encouragement of others.

Remember, it is not just stretcher issues that can destroy people. Many times it is the sense and feeling that no one is there who cares for me. The sense of feeling alone, helplessness in regards to something that you are dealing with in life. As someone once said to me, "I sit alone and wonder, how am I going to deal with this. It is so beyond me, my means, my ability. Who do I turn to?"

I also believe that as we minister, come alongside of people, God's power will enable you to think, to accomplish and assist in someway. It is written in Ephesians 3:20, "Now to Him who is able to do immeasurably more than all we ask or imagine, according to His power that is at work within us, to Him be glory in the church and in Jesus Christ throughout all generations, for ever and ever."

A SHOUT OF ENCOURAGEMENT

To you who are shouting for help and wondering if you are going to make it, keep your eyes, your faith and trust focused on God. Not on the circumstances or situations. Do not let time, issues, fear, hopelessness or that sinking feeling get the best of you. It might seem dark and time is running out, do not give into it. A great scripture of comfort and truth, "God will never leave you or forsake you. Come unto me all you that are weak and heavy laden and I will give you rest. Take my yoke upon you and learn from me, for I am gentle and humble in heart and you will find rest for your souls. For my yoke is easy and my burden is light."

Surround yourself with friends of encouragement. People who want to lift and care for you. It is alright to call out for help and assistance. We all go through stretcher times and could use some help.

For those of you who want to shout to others, keep your eyes on Jesus. It will call you to shout and minister to others. You will see and hear opportunities to encourage. You will waken to the fact that faith in Christ makes you want to be involved in the encouragement of others.

Please remember, God will empower you to accomplish ministry and assistance to others. For when Jesus calls you into ministry, He empowers you for that distinct ministry and task.

LETS SHOUT

What sound is coming from you, so others can hear? What sounds are coming from your church, week by week in regards to ministering to others? We need to be a bunch of shouters, with voices that carry words of encouragement and support. Voices that are calling out with hope and assistance to those who are wondering and hurting. Voices who offer involvement and hope. Voices who are saying, "even though you think you are not going to make it, I am here to shout louder, *WE ARE GOING TO MAKE IT.*"

T There's a rare and special quality in the way some people live

H However busy they may be, they still have the time to give

A Anything you ask or need, they will do their very best.

N No matter what the task is – or how simple the request

K Kindness just comes naturally to this rare and selfless few

S Special, giving people – people just like you!

This spells thanks. Thanks to all who care, lift, and shout.

"Grab a handle?"

"That's right. Grab a handle. Let's get started."

"Who? Me?"

"Yes, you! Okay, lift!"

"But how?" you ask. You've never been a stretcher-bearer before, and you wonder if you even have the potential to grab the handle on someone's stretcher. So let's talk about it.

First, do you believe in the concept of stretcher bearing? Because of what you have already read, you already have a better understanding of what stretcher bearing is, both as a concept and as a ministry. What are your own feelings about entering into a stretcher-bearing ministry yourself?

Are you beginning to realize how, at times within your own life, you could use stretcher-bearers, as well as be one to another person? Can you see the potential for ministry as well as feel the excitement? Do you see how everyone can benefit, including the kingdom of Jesus Christ? If these thoughts inspire you and if you feel enthusiastic about each possibility, then you are well on your way to becoming a stretcher-bearer.

Second, in order to increase your potential for grabbing the handles of a person's stretcher, there are three foundational concerns that need to happen in your life.

1. *You need to pray for sensitivity.* Pray for sensitivity to the world around you.

2. *You need to pray for creativity and imagination,* which is simply finding the means of showing someone you care.

3. *You need to live out this concept of stretcher bearing in your own life.* This way you can show others you also need encouragement and support at times. It helps

them not to feel embarrassed then, if they should need a stretcher-bearer.

Third, you need practical advice on how to grab the stretcher's handle. It literally can be just like lifting someone who is on a stretcher. Some of us don't think we can lift, but we usually can. The issue is that we don't always know how to lift and make our efforts work for the best.

Practical tips, however, can make that lifting easier. These tips will benefit both you as a carrier and the person who is on their stretcher. You will be able to start using many of these tips right away.

Let us now review the foundational elements of stretcher bearing and then conclude with practical tips on being a stretcher-bearer. After that I'm sure you will see that you have the potential to grab a handle today and be a stretcher-bearer.

FOUNDATIONAL ELEMENTS OF STRETCHER BEARING
Pray for Sensitivity

The ministry of a stretcher-bearer must begin by praying for sensitivity. This simply means asking God to make you aware of people and their needs. Ask Him to show you people who are in your area of outreach. Pray that you will be sensitive to their body language, which can be shown through feelings, emotions, facial expressions and attitudes.

At the beginning of each week, I pray that I might be sensitive to the needs of others and my prayer is basically as follows: "Lord, I give my eyes, my ears and my feelings about people to you. Lord, make my eyes see what You really want me to see. Make my ears hear what You want me to hear. Lord, make me sensitive to the feelings happening within myself, where You seem to give me understanding about others."

It is a simple prayer and the meaning and sincerity behind the prayer is what matters. And we begin to apply it by opening our eyes so we can see people. We need to see their facial expressions and be aware of what their body language is telling us. Perhaps their absence from certain situations indicates something is not as it should be. We need to look for those indicators, which can give us insights into people.

What kind of indicators do you see from your family, your friends and your neighbors? Are their smiles genuine or could they be hiding behind masks?

Many times we don't really see each other. This is often because we are not taking time to look in depth. We do not always notice in group situations who is absent. Our Lord saw people; He took the time to look at them. He could just look and sense the feelings people had.

We also need to listen. We need to hear both the words and the meanings people address to us. There is a sound even in the silence of others. Are we listening? Do we really listen to one another?

Young people who have come into my office to talk with me have told me, "My mom and dad don't listen to me. They talk to me, but they never talk with me." I had one young person say, "My mom and I had words today, except I didn't have a chance to use mine."

Since it is important that we pray for sensitivity, we must also pray for a keen awareness regarding our inward feelings. This would refer to the feelings we could perceive within ourselves as we talk with people. What are we feeling even as we are thinking of someone?

Have you ever had a certain person suddenly cross your mind? This can happen at a time when it makes little sense that you are even thinking of that person at all.

Have you ever awakened suddenly in the middle of the night with someone on your mind? But why then, when the clock is reading 2 A.M.? You would rather be sleeping, so why are you thinking of this person just then?

I believe that in these quiet, still moments God may choose to speak to us. And we need to respond right then to those sudden feelings that we have. If our intuition about another person wakes us up, we need to pray.

We are given a divine privilege by our Lord, that of "intercessory prayer." This is praying on behalf of others. Praying to our Lord about the experiences others may be going through now or in the future. I believe God often uses the sound of His own alarm to wake us up. He wants us to know about His love and concern for another person, and He wants our involvement.

Intercessory prayer is a very meaningful part in being a stretcher-bearer. When we feel we need to intercede, we first need to be sensitive and then respond with prayer in regard to these feelings we are having about a person.

Pray for Creativity and Imagination

Since you have decided you want to be a stretcher-bearer, your next step is to pray for creativity. This is simply, through the use of your imagination, showing someone, in a unique way that you care. You may wonder how you can show someone on a stretcher that in some unique way you care for that person.

For such times I pray for special direction; direction which allows me to minister to persons in a way they may especially need. It is meant as a practical means of showing persons that I am behind them, that I am thinking about them and that I am with them.

Sometimes, the creative things that come into my mind seem a little crazy, but they've opened up a very workable ministry. I will share some of my conclusions about them later.

Live It Out

The third foundational element in being a stretcher-bearer is simply to live out the concept within your own life. This means that, if at some time you are having difficulties that are hard, you must not only realize the importance of having stretcher bearers, but you also must allow them to minister to you.

If something has become quite real to you and you have been convinced of it, you will want to live it out fully. It is like being a witness of Jesus Christ. When Jesus has become real and personal to you, sharing this life-changing good news with others is something you just want to do. It is a natural expression because something wonderful touched your life.

I love my wife, and, if I were asked today to share things about that love, it would be very simple, because her love has touched my life. I want to tell people and show people that marriage can be beautiful and that marriage is worthwhile.

I remember hearing a statement by Lloyd Ogilvie, former pastor of Hollywood Presbyterian Church and chaplain of the United States Senate. He said, "Something has to happen to you before it can happen through you." In all my years of ministry, I have never forgotten that statement. I believe it is filled with tremendous truth – truth for us today and truth that we can apply in being stretcher-bearers. When you feel the importance of a stretcher-bearer ministering to you because of your own needs, you are then better prepared to be a stretcher-bearer to others.

A review of these three simple foundational elements needed in your life in order to be a stretcher-bearer are as follows:

1. Pray for sensitivity.
2. Pray for creativity.
3. Live it out. Live out the concept of stretcher bearing in you own life.

Now together, let's start learning how you can grab the handle and lift someone's stretcher.

PRACTICAL TIPS ON STRETCHER BEARING

When I was in the service, one of the highlights of my day was mail call. In Viet Nam, I would look forward to that helicopter dropping off its red bag of mail each day, because I needed to feel close to someone back home.

Letter writing, however, is not just for someone who is in the service. Nor is it just for people who are apart from us for some reason. Letter writing can also be a ministry of encouragement and support within a church.

Write Letters of Encouragement and Support

Each one of us loves to receive a personal letter, a letter that is "just for me." Perhaps it says simply, "I was thinking about you today and wanted to reach out and let you know my thoughts are with you." Such a letter is one of encouragement and support.

I started a program in my church of writing letters, simple letters of encouragement and support. First, I urged my staff to write two to three letters each week to people within the church. This would be a supportive measure, allowing people to know we were thinking of them.

Then I started a letter-writing program by the people within our congregation. Right now I have 60 people who write letters. They write at least one letter a week to someone.

Earlier, we talked about the different costs involved in being a stretcher-bearer. There is also a cost involved in writing letters of encouragement. The costs to be considered are your time, the stationery and the stamps.

The cost per letter is probably 55¢ for stationary and postage. There is a somewhat larger cost involved regarding your time. However, as there is more involved than just the letter, here are some simple steps, which I have included for you to follow:

1. *Take time to pray.* Pray for the Lord to direct you to the one who needs the letter.
2. *Take time to think.* Think about what difficulties this person may be having at this time.

3. *Once again turn to prayer.* Ask for guidance and for the right words to come into your mind that God intends for this person.

4. *Write your letter – any length from a few paragraphs to a page or two.* Don't worry about length.

5. *Address, seal and stamp the envelope and put it in the mail.*

Sometimes this one letter can be sufficient, but you need to be sensitive and open to God's leading spirit. He may continue to put this person within your heart and mind. Some people may continue to need your prayers, your notes and letters of encouragement and you will need to follow through and be supportive.

This is a wonderful ministry open to each one of us. Can you begin to imagine what would happen in your church if 50 people each wrote one letter a week? In one year that figure would reach 2,600 letters mailed. Doing this would take some time and some effort, but I truly believe that those letters would have a direct impact on the people who received them.

I know of people who have received these letters at a time when they needed them the most – just when they needed to know someone was behind them. In fact, these letters have sometimes been known to arrive at crucial or critical times. Whenever they arrive, however, they are more often than not received by a person who has need of a stretcher-bearer.

I want to share a personal letter I received from a dear man in our church family who had responded to the ministry of writing letters to others:

Dear Pastor Mike:

You can count on me! I'll be there every week with my letters. I think it's a great program. Even though I had heard you speak about the program before, I was very encouraged by your sermon on Sunday, and I hope my contributions will encourage you as well.

I pray that this program just gets bigger and better, because someday, somehow, somewhere, we all need to feel the love, encouragement and prayers of our brothers and sisters.

Praise God for the means even to be a stretcher-bearer. This could not happen without the love of our Lord for us and our love for Him.

Thank you, Lord, and you too, Pastor Mike, *for this opportunity to serve Him.*

Sincerely,

Bill Wasson[1]

Send Encouragement Cards

The people and staff of our church have so much faith in the ministry of letter writing that we have taken this concept and developed what we call "Encouragement Cards." We do this because we believe that Christians are people called to encourage other people in the name of Jesus Christ.

We give out Encouragement Cards once a month on "Encouragement Sunday," and we take the time to write short notes on them during our morning worship service. This ministry is so important to us that we use part of our worship service once a month to reach out to others.

On Encouragement Sunday, our specially designed postcards are inserted into the church bulletins. This way just about every person in the congregation receives one. An example of the design of an encouragement card is in the back of the book.

At the beginning of the service, the congregation is encouraged to pray for direction as to which persons might need these special notes. Then about halfway through the service and prior to the offering being taken, we pause. Everyone then is encouraged to write a card to someone. This person could be a friend, a relative or someone inside or outside the church family. While the congregation is writing, soft music plays in the background.

If the person you are writing to is a part of our church family, you simply write that name on the front of the card. The note itself is written on the back on the card. We next take the offering and at that time, people place their Encouragement Cards and offerings into the plate.

The next day, with the church providing the postage, one of our members, Susan, takes all these cards, addresses and stamps them. She then puts them into the Monday afternoon mail. Susan has found it has given her a tremendous opportunity for ministry.

We are a growing church with an attendance of about 300 people each Sunday morning. On an average, we figure that 175 cards are written by the congregation. It's encouraging to feel that along with the 175 cards in the church mail, another 100 are probably mailed by those taking their cards home.

So, along with the ones written by the staff members, we estimate that our church writes and sends over 300 Encouragement Cards each month. This five-minute effort during our worship service, one Sunday morning a month, has shown itself to be a powerful and effective ministry.

You have already seen the simplicity of our card. You are now better able to see how it can be used in your church service. I would like to encourage you and your church to become involved in this type of ministry. I would like to see you design a card similar to ours, then take those five minutes in your church service once a month and encourage people.

I want to tell you a story – one out of many – about a person whose life was touched by these cards. They had come just at the right time in her life.

I had gone to visit this dear lady in the hospital. She was still recovering after a period of being in intensive care. Most of her family does not live in this area and when I went to her room, she showed me something, which had already produced quite an impression upon her life.

Most people are familiar with the wheeled bedside tray found in nearly all hospitals. The main purpose of the tray is to allow the patient a suitable table from which to eat. Also, the water pitcher and glass are placed there. It's nice and handy because the patient can keep some personal items nearby and reach them easily, and that is what this lady had done. She excitedly took from her nearby tray eight different Encouragement Cards. They all had been written to her because she was in the hospital. The impact those cards had on her life made her feel loved, cared for and thought about. She had been very happy to see me, but I honestly believe that those cards had a more positive effect on her life that day than my own visit.

When I left the hospital, I felt really good inside, once again appreciating the ministry of stretcher-bearers. I realized fully just how many people in our church were actually touching the lives of others. I also realized that I, as a minister, was not called just to minister to others, but also to be a teacher, and example, so many others could learn to also minister within the life of another person. Encouragement Cards – they are a simple yet powerful tool for us to use, enabling us to grab a handle.

Share Candy and Gum

I don't know about you but I love to eat! I enjoy those moments when I can eat a good meal or even a snack. That probably explains why these next tips have a great deal to do with food and snacks.

Consider the ministry and outreach of candy bars and gum. If I want to show someone that I am really behind them, I have learned not only to write a letter to them, but also at times to include a piece of gum.

For instance, if I learn that someone is going through a hard time because of something that may have happened at work or school, I may feel they need some special encouragement. Later, perhaps after church, I might go up to them and say, "I am really behind you in prayer and I bought you a little gift just to show my support for you." The candy bar might be a Hershey or Snickers bar or any variety. It may be a whole pack of gum.

Now you may be thinking, "What if they don't like candy?" Or, "What if they don't like that kind of candy?" Or, "Perhaps they can't eat candy!"

Remember, such concerns are not the issue. It really doesn't matter what they do with those candy bars. What's important is the message it stands for. Such as, "I was thinking about you today in a very special way and I want to express my thoughts and my concern for you. So, I took the time and spent some of my money in order to buy you a little gift." You see, the price isn't important at all.

Candy Bars. Have you ever given a candy bar or a piece of gum to someone? It would amaze you how God can use it.

I remember one time when I received a letter from a dear friend of mine. He was going to school far away in the state of Kansas, and I was excited about receiving that letter. Inside, I found he had included a piece of Doublemint gum! After I read my letter, another friend walked into my office. He saw the letter and the gum. He asked, "Did that gum come in that letter today?"

I said, "Yes, it did."

Now to that enquirer, that was just a piece of gum and it probably looked like a crazy thing to do. To me, however, it was a lot more than a piece of gum. It was a bond between myself and my special friend in Kansas. A bond between stretcher-bearers who were encouraging and in support of one another. A bond that even miles could not separate. It was more than a piece of gum, you see, because it was friendship. It was togetherness. It was encouragement.

This type of support not only works, but it can be fun and enjoyable. It often brings a smile or even laughter to the person who is on the stretcher. One of the foundational elements of stretcher bearing is imagination and creativity, allowing you a practical means of showing someone you care in some unique way.

You have my word. If you start this ministry of giving candy bars and gum to people you are supporting, it will definitely have a tremendous impact upon their lives.

When I am invited to various churches or conferences to show them how to set up the ministry of stretcher-bearers, I always tell them about the example of candy bars. One thing I find especially exciting is that, by the end of the series, I always end up with a good many candy bars to take home.

I remember one church in particular where I had given these examples. They were so moved by the whole ministry of stretcher bearing that they gave me a special gift at the end of the session – four gigantic boxes of candy bars: M & M's with peanuts, Hershey bars, Milky Ways and Snickers. Each one of these four boxes held 36 candy bars. The people from this church had included a note saying, "We want to be a part of this ministry of outreach and encouragement to other people. Love the church family."

Those people from that church clearly understood that this whole concept could have a tremendous impact, and that is exactly what happened. I really enjoyed seeing special people who needed encouragement receive those candy bars.

Another way I gave out that candy was by going around to some of the children's Sunday School classes at our church. These were the real young ones, around kindergarten through fourth grade. I shared the candy bars and talked to these boys and girls. It was good for them to see that the pastor wanted to spend time with the younger-aged groups.

Yes, it really is a tremendous ministry, this ministry of candy bars. It's probably not too dietetic, but it does work as a very practical and enjoyable outreach.

Encouragement Candy Bar Sunday

Once a quarter in our church we hold encouragement candy bar Sunday. This takes place right after the morning worship service. Two tables are set up by our junior high or high school youth. I announce at the end of the service that today is encouragement candy bar Sunday. As you leave think of people within this church that you want to offer a token of encouragement. They might be on staff, a friend, or someone within the community here at the church. Go buy a candy bar or two and give it to them with a word of encouragement and appreciation either today or when you see them.

Each candy bar costs $1 and all proceeds go to our youth ministry. People flock to the tables and buy candy bars and share their appreciation of others, or maybe their support of them during stretcher times.

I remember one Sunday going up to our youth at the table and asked how they did on the candy bar sales. They told me that they sold over 400 candy bars in 15 minutes. I looked at them and said "that is so wonderful. Over 400 pieces of encouragement have been distributed to people. Your profit for the youth group is over $250. This is a fund raiser with two purposes accomplished. You have impacted our church community and youth group.

The attitude and feeling that comes over our church is so tremendous. People are smiling, encouraged, leaving church with a sense of giving and receiving. So much good done through a simple outreach of encouragement and support. I hope your church or business will pick up on this means of supporting and showing appreciation to others.

Hold a Family Altar

One of the most beautiful experiences of encouragement that I can share with you is the concept of Family Altar. This is a special time at our church and anyone in the church can participate: the Sunday School, the choir and even the youth groups.

We hold Family Altar at our church once a month, on a Sunday morning. During this time, people who want to pray at the altar in the front of the church are simply invited to come forward during the prayer time. First, they are encouraged to kneel before the Lord in order to give Him thanks for all the good things and the praises they feel within their own lives. It's an opportunity for them to come forward in a special way, because they feel they want to say "Thank you."

The second reason people are encouraged to come forward is regarding their personal needs and the issues they feel they want to bring before God. You see, many people who come to church on Sunday morning bring a great amount of excess baggage along with them. This baggage is full of emotional confusion, questions and heartaches as well as thoughts about decisions they must face during their coming week.

This baggage needs to be released and we offer people a time of encouragement. It's a special time when they can come before their Lord at the altar and just pray silently. There are no audible words spoken at the altar, there is only the sound of soft background music and people coming forward in order to kneel and pray.

The third part of this whole ministry is one of the most beautiful concepts of Family Altar. It is when others have the opportunity to encourage the people who are praying. If they see that a friend or a family member has come forward, they then get up from their seats and come to the altar as well. By kneeling behind their friends or family members, they are able to simply put a hand on their shoulders or take their hands and hold them, while they pray for them. No words are spoken at Family Altar, because it's just people supporting one another through a touch and by prayer.

If you were to come forward in order to encourage a person, you may know what that person's problem could be, and then again you may not know. It doesn't really matter, however. What matters is that person feeling the sensation of touch – not only of Jesus Christ – but that they feel the touch of Jesus Christ through another person. Friends, this is a powerful moment for them. These people don't feel alone because they feel accepted and strengthened.

At our church, Family Altar has now grown so large that I am unable to approach and touch a third of the people who come forward. I like to move around to as many as I can because, as their pastor, I want to put my hand on each shoulder and pray for each one.

Another support measure I try to use is, sometime during the next week, to write a letter of encouragement to as many people as I can of those who came forward to pray.

What I see that's so exciting is that, even though I am not always able to touch people, that's okay. You see, the real ministry is actually taking place right there among the people. People just like you and me, because we are all meant to minister to one another. We can all be stretcher-bearers. Once again I simply am the teacher of this concept, and it is a principle of stretcher bearing that works.

Family Altar means people coming forward. Some are discouraged, while others are there to encourage and to pray for one another, through a supportive ministry. Simply praying in silence before the Lord.

After a few minutes of silent prayer, either my associate or I will close this special time by thanking the Lord for these moments and these people. During this closing prayer, people begin to make their way back to their seats. Some wait until the end of prayer, then simply stand up and return. But all are encouraged before God and through the touch of others.

When we first began Family Altar, many were hesitant about going forward. But now that people are more familiar with this part of the service, they no longer feel shy, embarrassed or ashamed. They just want to be on their knees before God. Many go back to their seats with tears. Tears which allow them to relieve some of their emotional stress. Some go back smiling, because they feel they are truly being cared for. Family Altar is a beautiful moment. It is people encouraging one another in prayer – a special time each month in the congregational life of our church.

Basket of Love

This is an outreach we do at the church to people who have a family member going into surgery. Have you ever noticed that to the people that are having a surgery or medical procedure done, encouragement is given thru prayer, cards, flowers or a visit to the hospital.

But I began to think as wonderful as that is what about the family that is going through the procedure with a loved one. What about them sitting in a waiting room, wondering about the outcome of the surgery and passing the time till they receive word. I thought here is an avenue of encouragement that is needed.

With that in mind we designed baskets of encouragement. On the night before a surgery is planned I make some people in our church aware of the time and hospital. They then put together a basket. The basket consists of four bottles of water, some fruit, little packages of nuts and crackers, a few candy bars (you must have candy bars) a people magazine and a card of encouragement and prayer.

The basket is delivered by the people personally to the family sitting in the waiting room. They walk up to them and explain that this is from your church family to let you know our prayers and concern are with you and your loved one. As you wait for the results, please snack on something, drink some water. As you reach into the basket this will affirm our support for you and your family today.

They need support as well as the one going through the procedure and so many times we forget them. The look on their face is so wonderful when the basket is given to them and explained its purpose. I have been in many waiting rooms with families and have witnessed the arrival of the basket and the impact it has had on so many. They are moved, encouraged and appreciate their church.

One additional observation I have noticed many times. There are other people waiting for the outcome of their loved ones. They watch what has happened to the people of our church and they too are moved. No one else is receiving anything.

So many times our people have shared goodies from the basket with others in the waiting room. What an outreach and testimony to them about our church, caring for one another and trusting in our Lord. A sense of community and support takes place right at the hospital.

The cost of the basket runs around $15. I have two couples who are in charge of this ministry so that it assures someone is available to deliver the basket. If for some reason both cannot, then I will take the basket to the family on behalf of the church.

ENJOY BREAKFAST OR LUNCH WITH SOMEONE

Remember when I told you before that I love to eat? It's true, and I want to share another practical tip that has to do with eating.

If people have the desire to be stretcher-bearers and want to become involved within the lives of others, I encourage them to have breakfast, lunch or dessert with someone once a month.

The only way you really get to know a person is by taking the time to be with them and to talk together. When you are with people talking, it is normal for conversation to flow freely back and forth. I have learned that neutral settings such as restaurants are great places to go. You can meet for breakfast, or lunch or at any convenient time in the day, for say, a piece of pie and a cup of coffee. Restaurants can create a good atmosphere for conversation and for friendships to develop.

As you get better acquainted and these friendships become more meaningful, people will begin to be more open with one another and to feel comfortable in saying, "I need to feel your support, can you pray for me this week?" Then, once again we are able to see the concept of stretcher bearing taking place.

Using myself as an example, I probably eat either a breakfast or a lunch with different people, six or seven times each week. They are people within, or outside, the church membership. These times with them are never intended as a way of persuading a person to do a job within the church, like being a Sunday School teacher or youth counselor. I simply do not work in that way. The reason I go out with people is because I want to get to know them and I want to show people that I care about them.

I often find I have to travel to their offices or the areas where they are working, but that's fine. I quite frankly enjoy doing this, because I am then able to see part of their everyday world. It gives me another opportunity to show people I am concerned about them as persons, and it has nothing to do with their work or participation in church matters or their financial support. I only want each one to understand that I am interested in him or her as a person, because I am a person and we need one another.

Once again you will find there is a cost involved, regarding your time and energy. You also will need to have the necessary funds to go to lunch or breakfast. Many times when you eat with someone, it is Dutch treat; sometimes you will want to buy the other person's meal, and oftentimes he or she will wish to buy yours.

We need to be reminded of the questions again: Is it worth the effort? Do you get what you pay for? I know personally that the opportunities are there, both for developing friendships as well as for enhancing the ministry of stretcher bearing. I do know that I am totally sold on the idea.

I remember one year when I received a call from the Department of Internal Revenue. They wanted me to come in and explain the deductions I had claimed for breakfasts and lunches. Against the salary I was making, it seemed to be totally out of proportion. I went to see them and I not only took all my receipts, but I also brought my daily calendar for that year. I had always written my costs down upon it each day.

The man from the Internal Revenue Service and I totaled all my figures. When we were through, he could hardly believe it. He said, "You're not lying, you really do believe in this ministry of encouraging people."

I said, "Oh yes, I really do and I'm going to do the same thing again this year."

When I walked out of their office, I was a happy man. For one thing, I didn't owe them any more money, and they were able to see that this ministry was really a true conviction of mine.

I now have many people within my church who spend time having these special breakfasts and lunches with others. There is also a fairly large group of people who go to lunch together each Monday. I join this group just as often as I can and so do members of my staff, including the church secretaries. Many people are a part of this out-to-lunch bunch. It is a fun group, a group of people who like to laugh and talk with each other. But what's so beautiful is that we are strengthening friendships, which allow us to be stretcher-bearers in times of need.

What might keep you from taking someone out to breakfast? What about a lunch or dessert with someone? Yes, it does take a little effort and a little money as well, because you probably will have to pick up some checks. But, my friends, it works. It's a good solid handle to hold in your stretcher-bearing ministry.

PARTICIPATE IN SUPPORTIVE FELLOWSHIP

Within my own heart, I am quite convinced that there is simply no way for people to make it socially, spiritually and psychologically if they choose to go through life setting themselves apart from others. We all need other people. We need people in our lives who can touch us in ways that are positive. Personally, I feel very fortunate that so many people around me are supportive and have become such a source of encouragement to me.

Specifically, I am involved in what is called "supportive fellowship." This is an intimate group of people who gather together at a designated time – a group of people who are committed to one another through the love they share for their Lord, Jesus Christ. We are supportive so we can be a source of strength to one another, as we each strive to live out our relationship with God within this world. Paul said in Galatians 6:2 (*KJV*), "Bear ye one another's burdens, and so fulfill the law of Christ."

Remember how, in the story of the four stretcher-bearing friends, they were intimately supportive of their friend on the stretcher? This is an excellent example of a supportive fellowship. It is people who are committed to one another.

Ideally, the number of people involved in a supportive fellowship group should be from two to four people. I do not believe it should include more than that number. A supportive fellowship group could meet once a week, once every two weeks or once a month, whichever the group feels is best.

As you meet, your purpose is to be supportive of one another. Your meetings could take place in a home, at a restaurant or anywhere that is acceptable to each member of the group. When you meet you must be willing to be vulnerable to each other. Remember, you meet to support one another as you each strive to live your life out there within the real world. You meet in affirmation of one another, affirming the successes as well as being in support through frustrations, and helping to develop the growth you are each reaching for within your life.

Supportive fellowship is used to hold each other accountable. Accountable to be God's person and accountable to follow through on your dreams and desires. You are also accountable to be in prayer for one another, meaning that you are consistently supportive in prayer.

There is a question I would like you to consider. Can you name three or four people that pray for you each day? People who are supportive of you, for the person you are and are becoming in God? Supportive fellowship can open the door for prayer partners to become part of your life.

Supportive fellowship is allowing yourself to be vulnerable. It is being with the people who can share your successes and your failures. Where you can be open and never have to hide behind a mask. If you feel like crying, you can cry. If you feel like sharing an accomplishment, you need to have people who can accept you for who you are and what you have become.

Dave Burns – My Support

For the last eight or nine years, I have been very fortunate to be part of a supportive fellowship group. I cannot tell you the exact date when ours began, but it started with a man whom I call "my roof cutter." His name is Dave Burns.

Dave and I began to meet with one another because we believed we needed each other. We believed that if we were going to be the men of God that God intended us to be, we needed to be accountable, vulnerable and to feel supported. We truly felt we could be used for that source of encouragement and support in one another's growth in life.

When all this began eight or nine years ago, we lived only 10 minutes apart. Each Friday we gathered at a certain restaurant and spent time talking with each other. We would talk about what was happening within our own lives, how our individual growth seemed to be developing and things such as that.

We met like this for about two or three years and then, because of changes in our ministry, we found we were about half an hour apart. We were each established at different churches in different cities, but we decided upon a new plan. Every Friday for one month I would drive into his city where we met at a restaurant. Then the following month, he drove into my city and we met at a restaurant there. We were still able to be supportive and encouraging and we were both still growing. We were not only growing in our ministries, but as husbands, as sons and as friends to others in the areas of responsibility where God had us placed in life.

This pattern continued for a few more years. Then Dave was called to a church, which was over an hour away from where I was living. We knew there would have to be changes so it was decided we would meet every two weeks on a Thursday. He now drives part way and I also drive part way. We meet at a restaurant halfway between. Once again, we are still able to be supportive to one another. I firmly believe if either one of us were called to a church out of state, Dave and I would still figure out a way to meet together in support, even if it were only once or twice a year.

It honestly makes me feel good to tell you that these breakfasts we share are so uplifting. We both feel excited about the things we are able to share and hear. When we leave, I usually feel so thankful and good inside for this time we have had.

Admittedly, there are times when I don't want to get out of bed that early to go have breakfast, times when I'm tired and worn out and would much rather sleep. Sometimes when we get through eating, I realize that no real issues were discussed that day, nothing phenomenal happened and no particularly uplifting experiences took place. There are also times when I would rather not fight the traffic driving the freeway, even meeting halfway, but still I know I will continue to do this.

The reasons I will continue are because I need Dave as my special friend, I need discipline, and I need encouragement in my life from Dave Burns. I believe, for all these same reasons, Dave also needs me. I know that whatever the cost involved to be a stretcher-bearer to one another, we will pay that cost. I truly believe this.

I wanted to share these honest feelings with you because it is important for you to understand that sometimes we need to let ourselves be disciplined. We need to feel so convicted of what we believe, that no matter what we might experience contrary to this, we must continue to go forward under God's direction. We must have the faith to know He would have us benefit from the experience. I know that, for me, the discipline and accountability have been excellent, because I need these strengths within my life.

Dave and I still need this support today. I can see this bond between us constantly growing. I think we will probably continue to meet like this until one of us should die. Perhaps – who knows – someday when both of us are there in heaven, we will probably still meet for breakfast, maybe for eternity.

CONCLUSION

Through the use of your own imagination and creativity, I feel you could probably think of some more practical tips that could be inserted here. You see, as long as we continue the work of stretcher bearing, I believe God continues using our imagination and creativity in showing us practical and unique ways of letting others know how much we care for them.

I sincerely hope that many of the tips found here make sense, that they make such good sense that you feel even stronger about being a stretcher-bearer. I hope you now can say, "I know I can grab that handle and lift! It will take effort but I can do it."

I will repeat what I said previously. You can start today. There is probably someone who could use a letter from you right now. Perhaps there is someone who might want to go out to breakfast. Is there anyone you can think of who would enjoy that special candy bar or piece of gum? I believe you could name such people.

Think about Family Altar. Could you suggest this ministry and talk it over within your church groups, at your board meetings or in your Sunday School classes? I encourage you in this because I know it works. All these ideas work well to help other people.

I ask that you take a moment to pray for God's leading in your life. Pray that you will begin to think of hurting people that you can reach, you can help. Pray that God will continue to bring people to your mind over the next few months and years that need their burdens carried and their stretcher lifted.

You see, stretchers can be lifted. We just need someone to grab the handle. I truly pray for that someone to be you. God bless you, and may the suggestions I was able to share through these pages not only work, but also give you the same blessings I have received within my own life.

PERSONAL TIME

Right now, take a couple of minutes to write a card or letter of encouragement to someone God has placed on your mind. Your written words of encouragement can be the touch from our Lord that so many need.

GRAB A HANDLE

I pray that our time together has showed you the power and potential of the ministry of encouragement.

I believe stretchers can be lifted. We just need to grab the handle and know how to lift. I truly pray that you will be one of the lifters. God bless you, stretcher-bearer.

Note

1. Used by permission.

PERSONAL TALLY SHEET

Name of person on a stretcher: _____

Problem: _____

_____

WHAT'S THE REAL ISSUE?

Friend and Issue　　　　　　　　*How I Can Build Trust*

1. _____　　1. _____

　　_____　　　　_____

2. _____　　2. _____

　　_____　　　　_____

3. _____　　3. _____

　　_____　　　　_____

BECOMING A PAIR OF SCISSORS

Main Issues　　　　　　　　　*Secondary Issues*

(Use this page as a master copy for making additional copes, so you can have a completed tally sheet for each person whose stretcher you are willing to bear.)

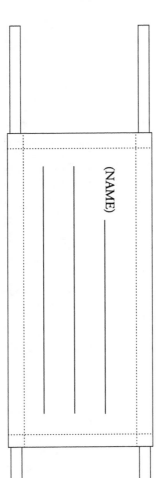

Place your organization's name and address here

(NAME)

SUPPORTING ONE ANOTHER

" ...and let us consider how to stimulate one another to love and good deeds, not forsaking our own assembling together, as is the habit of some, but **encouraging one another**; and all the more, as you see the day drawing near. "

Hebrews 10:24-25

STRETCHER BEARER MINISTRIES

ADDITIONAL RESOURCE MATERIALS

The Book, *The Stretcher* $15

"Becoming A Stretcher Bearer" Self Study Manual $35
Includes workbook and entire seminar on CD

"Becoming A Stretcher Bearer" Audio Series......................$20
Includes highlights from the seminar on CD

For more resources and to place an order, please visit our website.

SEMINAR INFORMATION

Pastor and author Michael Slater travels the U.S. speaking on the ministry of Support and Encouragement at churches, retreats, colleges, and organizations. For more information on our "Becoming A Stretcher Bearer" seminar or to book Pastor Mike for your next speaking engagement, please visit our website.

CONTACT INFORMATION

P.O. Box 1035
La Habra, California 90633-1035

(714) 869-1440 | mike@stretcherbearerministries.org

www.stretcherbearerministries.org

CPSIA information can be obtained
at www.ICGtesting.com
Printed in the USA
FSHW01n0558290818
51643FS

9 780983 204305